Conversations with the Homeless

# CONVERSATIONS
## *with the* HOMELESS

### Stephen Pernotto

STEVE PERNOTTO PUBLICATIONS

CONVERSATIONS WITH THE HOMELESS
Stephen Pernotto

Printed in the United States of America.

Steve Pernotto Publications
sppublications@carolina.rr.com

Trade Paperback 978-1-4675-8411-1
E-book 978-1-4675-8412-8

Cover design by Kelly Leslie
Book design by Catherine Leonardo

This edition was prepared for printing by The Editorial Department
7650 E. Broadway, #308, Tucson, Arizona 85710
www.editorialdepartment.com

# Introduction

IN WRITING THIS COLLECTION OF STORIES of my conversations with the homeless, I have three objectives
in mind. The first is to let readers see and hear the
homeless from a firsthand perspective. Most people
don't know much about the lives and struggles of the
homeless and are afraid of them. They shouldn't be.
Homeless people are the most vulnerable people in
the community. Second, I want to spotlight the great
work being done by the organizations that work with
the homeless. They are generally not government-
managed. The Urban Ministry, where I volunteer, is

# Introduction

one of those organizations. Although there are guidelines we use to help the homeless deal with problems, when in doubt about a situation, we lean towards compassion. The third objective is to raise money for the continued work of The Urban Ministry. All proceeds from this book will be given to the Urban Ministry to continue and expand its important role in the community in Charlotte North Carolina.

The book is a compilation of conversations and counseling sessions with more than 100 homeless people I worked with over the course of three years. Their names are changed and every attempt has been made to ensure they can't be specifically identified. The stories, conversations and responses are accurate and real. The struggles associated with homelessness captured in this book are representative of the most basic needs of our society; food, clothing, shelter, medical care, and survival on the streets as the day-to-day attempt to meet these needs sucks the energy out of most people. Yet somehow they find a way to carry on, plodding their course, celebrating small victories as an Olympian would celebrate a gold medal. The stories are a window into the lives of the homeless on the streets of Charlotte, NC. There are few happy endings whereby someone gets out of the cycle, and the stories can become numbing in their consistency. However, there are many happy occasions when

# Introduction

someone has a small win and becomes reenergized and motivated. Don't let the stories numb you to the people. They represent life on the streets, as it exists today.

The Urban Ministry is an interfaith organization in Charlotte, North Carolina, that helps poor and homeless people. A soup kitchen serves lunch 365 days a year. At Urban Ministry, the term "neighbor" is used to refer to the people who come through the doors. Lunch is the catalyst to bring homeless neighbors in the area to the Center. Urban Ministry offers a number of other services, including showers, laundry, mail, counseling with referrals, enrichment programs, substance abuse treatment, and community education. All of this is designed to help people survive and eventually take steps to find employment and permanent housing.

The soup kitchen first opened in 1979 at St. Peter's Episcopal Church and moved in 1994 to the Urban Ministry Center, where it has been in continuous operation ever since. People can receive a hot, nutritious lunch with no questions asked or prerequisites for service. During its 30-year history, despite ice storms, heat waves, power outages, and ever-increasing demand, never once did it fail to deliver lunch to people. In 2011, 103,414 lunches were served, a five-percent increase over 2010.

The 39 staff members at Urban Ministry

are dedicated to providing a warm and welcoming environment. Volunteers are the mainstay of the Center; hundreds of them support and manage each of the services, all of them trying to make some small difference in a neighbor's life. The soup kitchen operates with a different volunteer crew each day, over 300 volunteers each month, under the direction of a full-time manager and part-time assistant. Some people have been volunteering at the Urban Ministry for more than 20 years.

I work at Urban Ministry weekly as a volunteer counselor. The counseling isn't therapeutic; in most cases, it may be better described as coordinating. The majority of it is primarily aimed at obtaining official ID for neighbors, prescription assistance, food, transportation, emergency housing, and other referrals. However, often people just want to talk or have deep-rooted issues they wish to air, and a dose of real counseling comes into play.

The Urban Ministry does not encourage dependency in any way. The desire is to help people become self-sufficient and less dependent upon the community. Small wins for the homeless are powerful, as I had a chance to see while counseling at The Urban Ministry. I haven't met a neighbor who expected all of his or her problems to end after meeting with a counselor. Instead, they want to take a step forward, whatever forward means to them. In almost every case, that small step is enough to motivate and continue to propel them forward.

There are four counseling rooms, and number three is my preferred room. They are Spartan with different shades of gray abundant throughout. Entering number three, you notice the back wall is painted the deepest shade of gray. A window overlooking the parking lot and community garden breaks up the dullness and brings some light into the space. The other three walls are painted a lighter shade of gray that reminds me of smoke. The commercial carpet, with its tones of gray and brown, looks dirty and makes you to want to run a vacuum over it. In the left-hand corner, beneath a welcome sign taped to the wall, sits a small file cabinet that holds phone books and whatever else someone wants to stash out of sight. The desk is positioned on the right side against the wall. An old computer squats on the desk next to a scanner. Two stationary chairs, one against the back wall and one against the left wall, and a chair on wheels in front of the desk complete the furniture arrangement.

The book is organized into eight chapters. The first seven reflect the main reason why, in my opinion, the individuals in the chapter are homeless at that time. The stories in Chapter 8, along with the neighbors' reasons for homelessness, were impossible for me to categorize. I don't attempt to get at the

# Introduction

core reason for someone's homelessness; I'll leave
that to others to theorize. It's important to realize
that homelessness is rarely caused by one factor act-
ing independently. Generally, the problems come in
groupings such as prison sentences, joblessness, and
substance abuse. I hope you come away with an en-
lightened perspective of the struggles associated
with homelessness.

# 1

# Looking for Work

## *Mike*

HE LOST HIS JOB 12 MONTHS AGO, and since then his life has been spinning out of control. Three months ago Mike was living in a four-bedroom home on the north side of town with his wife and two children; for the last two months he's lived in the men's shelter. His wife asked for a separation, and he stayed with a friend for a month before moving into the shelter. He talks about how he counseled homeless at another organization, and many of the people at the shelter are his former clients, some of whom he saw downstairs at

1

lunch today. He suffers from type 2 diabetes, and his current lifestyle doesn't help him manage the situation—he eats what's available whenever he can find food.

The recent trauma in his life has taken a psychological toll on his mood. He's depressed and sees a doctor at the behavioral health clinic. It looks as though his doctor isn't sure what's wrong, gives some latitude on a diagnosis, and prescribes medications for depression, bipolar disorder, and schizophrenia.

Mike treats his chair like a hot stove, constantly moving around and shuffling his feet on the floor as if late for an appointment. He has no income and needs assistance to pay for the medications. I give him a voucher for them and two bus passes to go to the clinic today and begin his regimen. It will take a few weeks for the medication to kick in, and I advise him not to expect an immediate change, which he acknowledges. He spends some time talking about his children, two stepdaughters and two sons of his own. He describes his older son as a star high school baseball player with a college scholarship prospect. He smiles for the first time. "Boy's got a wicked fastball."

While talking about his children, Mike's spirit seems to drift out of the room. I sense he may be on the verge of breaking down and ask if he wants to go to the hospital. His head shakes slowly back and forth as he struggles to get up. "It's time I go." He walks toward the door. I stand and shake his hand. I don't have words to soothe his sorrow but I wish him well and advise him to come back anytime he wants to talk to someone. He seems embarrassed and confused; emotions ranging from timid hope to grief and deep anxiety flit across his face as he leaves.

# Bob

Why is Bob still looking for work? I met him last year when he came to UMC for the first time, and he was looking for work then. He sent his résumé to a number of firms and asked if I could help with Gmail to see if he had any responses. There were none. I offer to review his résumé, make suggestions, and rework it with him. If needed I'll retype it for him and leave the updated version in his mailbox on Tuesday, along with a copy on a disc.

He has a strong background in the restaurant business, having worked in restaurants his entire career, starting as a busboy and working his way up to executive chef at his last location. He has rave references from all his former employers. We discuss food, and he talks about how much he likes his work. He has a lot of perseverance and tenacity and is dealing as best he can with his homelessness and the adversity it brings. I find no obvious answers to why he hasn't found a job, other than the poor economy and his homeless environment, which could influence his behavior and ultimately his chances to land a job.

Two men's shelters in Charlotte are run by the same agency. He stays at the shelter on Statesville Street, not far from the other on North Tryon. Surprisingly, he remarks how much better the Statesville location is than the Tryon location. He talks about drug dealing, theft, and fights as common occurrences at Tryon. This is a change, since Statesville has traditionally been more troublesome and is often referred to by neighbors as the "dog pound."

I ask, "What changed?"

"There's a new manager at Statesville. He made some changes for the better, especially the cleanliness of the place. When you go to do number two, you don't have to worry about pee on the seat anymore."

We shake hands and I wish him well. I follow up, type his reworked résumé at home, and leave a paper copy and a disc in his mailbox the next day.

# Rich

He seems distracted and a bit frantic as he enters the room. He walks in, sits down, and immediately calls someone on his phone but doesn't get an answer. He glances quickly out the window as if in thought, still without looking at me or saying hello.

"Are you expecting a call?" I ask.

"I'm supposed to meet someone later and I can't reach them."

I try to get his full attention. "What would you like to talk about?" He settles back and begins talking. He has a good chance at a job this week but needs to work through a deal-killing problem that stands in front of it. I spoke with Rich a year ago when he was close to a job offer as a truck driver. He applied for his commercial driver's license then but was not approved because he is nearsighted and needs corrective lenses. He has another interview for a driving job in two weeks.

"I need this job. I been working on it for a while, and now it may fall through because of a pair of glasses." If he applies for an eye exam and eyewear through the Lions Club, it will take approximately four months before the exam is scheduled and another two weeks to get the eyewear. I don't have another option top of mind so we toss around ideas and thoughts. We both agree he should apply to the Lions Club as a safety net, so I leave the room to fax it. When I return, he's finishing a conversation with his girlfriend. She suggests he try for a free exam at Walmart today and if successful, get his eyewear donated from LensCrafters.

"That's a great idea," I say, "and I bet it could all happen within your timeframe—and for free." We're both excited. I give him a verification letter to bring to Walmart that says we're working with him and he's homeless. If they do the exam, we can schedule an appointment with LensCrafters for the eyewear. As he's leaving the office he asks if I could check the fax machine to see if a job application has been sent from the trucking company. We go together and find the application waiting for him. That puts a big smile on his face. This looks like a win for Richard.

Because I am a volunteer and appointments aren't made by neighbors for a specific counselor, I don't see the same people regularly. I won't be able to follow up with Richard when he needs someone regarding his job application or the glasses.

He leaves the office area upbeat and excited, and his enthusiasm is contagious.

## Paul

Paul is a walking time bomb. His blood pressure is 200 over 90, placing him deep within stroke territory. He lived from paycheck to paycheck for three years, residing in a motel room, until he lost his job. Shortly afterwards, he was forced to leave the motel and live on the streets.

"It didn't have to be this way," he says, "but I made some lousy choices in my life and now at sixty years old, I'm homeless." He doesn't care to go into detail about the choices. Tonight will be different for him because of the Room at the Inn program. It's a seasonal program run by local churches from December to March. Church vans pick up participants at UMC each evening and bring them to a participating church. Generally there are over 100 cots available each night, but not enough to guarantee everyone a place to sleep. Women and children are first in the triage, followed by older men down to the youngest. Paul has a very good chance of being selected for participation at one of the local churches because of his age.

He also needs assistance getting prescription medications for his high blood pressure. Since he hasn't been here in a while, we review other services that will be important to him such as the daily lunch program, employment assistance, counseling, transportation, and nurse services.

I offer him two passes to go the emergency room tonight, but he doesn't want to risk losing a space with Room at the Inn. I urge him to come in tomorrow to see the nurse. Paul thanks me for the information and promises to see the nurse tomorrow morning. We stand, shake hands, and he leaves to get into line.

# Don

The first time I met Don, he needed transportation to Jacksonville, NC, for a long-term construction job offered to him through a day-labor pool. I recall the phone conversation I had with the day-labor coordinator to ask if she could help with a ride to the site. "I can try but can't commit." Ultimately, she couldn't make it happen. In 2009 he came to Charlotte from out of state with a job, but after it ended, he was unable to find work, became homeless, and began staying at the men's shelter.

Don is a sincere guy who recently completed a construction course through goodwill industries and is again working hard to get a job. I review his résumé and suggest he network with people who know his work and could recommend him. He's hopeful of landing a job with a firm constructing a new building downtown, and he thinks the Democratic primary coming to Charlotte in 2012 will enhance his chances because of the additional construction projects that will be tied to it. "I know ten guys at the shelter who've landed jobs recently in construction on a downtown project." This type of news is great to hear.

He showed me some court papers. "I'm on a three-month probation, failure to pay child support." He feels the judge was a little rough on him. He needs bus passes to get back and forth to a temporary job this week. He also needs decent reading glasses; his pair of cheap ones bother him and make his eyesight worse. I complete a Lions Club request and give him six bus passes with directions to buy his own when he gets paid. More than anything else, he needs a permanent job.

# Ken

When I first meet him I know something's wrong. His eyes are hollow, staring at nothing in particular as if he's somewhere else. As we walk upstairs, he says he's close to being evicted from his apartment. In the office, he slumps into the chair and leans forward with his elbows on his knees and his hands folded. He continues to look down. "I'm hungry, I'm cold, and I'm close to being on the streets." His voice is soft and low. He lives in his own apartment now but lost his job as a janitor a few weeks ago. His former employer wanted him and another man to clean a large restaurant and kitchen in two hours. The timeframe was too short to properly clean a restaurant of that size, and besides, the bus fare to the site would eat up 20 percent of his pay, so he declined the job. His employer never called him back.

We discuss his food situation. "You can get a week's supply of groceries from Loaves and Fishes," a charity that gives food to the homeless, which perks him up a little. We begin to prepare the L&F request when I ask his birth date.

He laughs. "I'm not sure." He lied about his age in middle school to get a driver's license, and the confusion mounted over the years as he continued to lie about his age to get jobs. He doesn't have a birth certificate and his parents are gone. He thinks his birth year is 1955, 1956, or 1957. We both have a good laugh over this. He says, "I haven't laughed in a long time."

I arrange the L&F referral and direct him to crisis assistance for clothing. I don't have a good idea or option to avoid the eviction. "Come back on Wednesday and enroll in the jobs program. Labor positions are sometimes available, and you could qualify for one." He may be able to hold off the landlord if he has future income lined up. It's a ray of hope but not much else. He thanks me, we shake hands, and he leaves the office.

# Eddie

Three months ago, Eddie left his wife and two children in Michigan and came to Charlotte to find work but hasn't been successful. He stayed with two friends for a while, but they left town, and Eddie's now living on the streets. He stayed at Room at the Inn last night and will try to get another placement tonight. He cracked the cartilage in his kneecap jumping from a wall and now is walking with a limp. The time living on the streets, the injury to his knee-cap, and his unsuccessful effort to find work have him scared. He wants to go back home to his family and needs bus fare to get there.

"Comin' here like this is one of the biggest mis-takes I ever made." He leans forward in his chair and looks down at the floor. "The only thing worse was the time I robbed a place when I was about 26 and spent 18 years in prison for it. Let me out in '03." We look up the bus fare on the Greyhound site—$139. Normally Travelers Aid will pay half if an individual has been in town for less than three months and has a verifiable destination. They prefer the rider come up with the other half.

I push the phone across the desk to him. He calls his wife and discusses his decision with her. She wants him home but doesn't have any money to send him. Sometimes in situations like Eddie's, Travelers aid will give him the whole bus fare.

I give him a referral from UMC and a map to Travelers Aid and shake his hand. "If you don't get the other half, come back. No promises, but we may be able to help."

# Brian

Brian, born in Liberia, is a Navy veteran with a green card and a Social Security card. New to Charlotte, he decided to stay in North Carolina and get a job. He looks out the gray room's window at the bright day. "Charlotte's a good place to raise a family, my wife and kids will enjoy it here." He'll need a North Carolina ID. His wife and two children live elsewhere, and he plans to bring them to Charlotte when he gets a job. Currently he's staying with friends. I hand him a Department of Motor Vehicles (DMV) waiver, which will waive the fee for his ID.

I tell him, "I'd also like you to call the VA office and make an appointment to learn about benefits you're entitled to as a vet."

"I will." He stands and extends his hand.

This seems like an easy one. But you never know.

# Steve

Steve lasted one day on his new job. He had to quit because his fiancée of four months left him and he lost his transportation (her car) to and from work, along with their shared motel room. He's now staying at the men's shelter.

"What happened?" I ask. "Did she just get up and leave and not say anything?"

He exhales deeply and settles back in his chair. "No, it was me. She just couldn't put up with my moods anymore. Told me she'd had enough."

I lean back. "Moods?"

He has a litany of issues he's dealing with that cause mood swings, and he now wants to work on them all at the same time. He's bipolar, suffers from depression, and has type 2 diabetes. He quit taking medication for his mental health two months ago and can't follow a diet for his diabetes due to his living conditions and itinerant lifestyle. He's also a substance abuser and heavy smoker. I silently wonder how she stayed with him for four months. Now he wants to turn his life around on all fronts at once, a tall order for anyone.

"Do you really feel you have the determination and discipline to work on all these goals at the same time?"

"All the way." He has three doctor appointments in the next two weeks to help him get started. He needs transportation to each. It's hard to tell how this will all eventually play out. He's most upset about his fiancée leaving him, and I think that more than anything else is driving him to change his lifestyle. He realizes he's going to have to maintain his focus, and he has a history of not being able to do that. First, he needs to get back on his meds. He'll also need some mentorship, professional help, and support. Fortunately for him, his family has offered to help him if he evens out his moods.

"First step, you should focus on stabilizing your emotional health. Once that's under control, it'll be much easier to tackle the rest. Go see your family and let them know your plans. I have a feeling they'll like what they hear and help you along. Also let your fiancée know what you're doing. Ask her to give you some time."

He listens intently, nodding with each point. On second thought, I write down his tasks in order of priority and hand him the list. I also give him the bus passes for the doctor visits. With the right help, discipline, and some luck, I think he can turn this around.

# Ray

Ray is new to the area and stays at the men's shelter. He asks if we can help him find work. I like him immediately. He's outgoing and seems determined to land a job.

"Any felony convictions?"

He shakes his head. "I stay away from that stuff."

He shows me his résumé, and I make a few suggestions and suggest he retype it. "Go to the library. They have computers and printers you can use. Then come back Wednesday for the job-coaching program. I'll be here and can print copies of your résumé." He nods and takes notes while I talk.

"Got a cigarette?" he asks.

"I don't smoke cigarettes, but I do smoke cigars. I'll bring you a couple on Wednesday." I hope this will give him added incentive to show up and collect.

Wednesday, Ray shows up at the jobs program, and I hand him two cigars. He thanks me for remembering. He's anxious to begin work on his job plan. He's a smart guy with a clean record, making it easier to place him in a job and get him out of the shelter. One of the volunteer job counselors is assigned to help him update his résumé on a web-based program. I sit and listen while they work together. She's spectacular in the way she explains, exhibits patience, and brings him along. From the professional manner in which she conducts and leads the session, I suspect she's a teacher. Afterwards, I ask her and she confirms she is indeed a high school teacher with 13 years' experience. Ray's coming back Friday to follow up with her. I feel he's on the right track to meet his objective.

I meet with Ray again later in the week to discuss his job search. To my surprise, he hasn't begun the process. He says it's because he doesn't have a NC ID and won't be able to get a job until he gets one. "You could apply for jobs without an ID and get started," I say. "What's the holdup?"

He doesn't respond to this question. Instead he tells me his temporary driver's permit expired the day before. I give him a DMV waiver and ask him to go to there today to get his permanent driver's license. If he's clean, as he says he is, he has a great chance of breaking out of the homeless cycle. He realizes I'm a little frustrated at his lack of initiative. We agree to meet again on Monday.

While he's sitting with me, I call an employer I know and ask about maintenance openings in their headquarters building. I learn they outsource their maintenance work, and I get the number of the firm they use and ask Ray to call them. He seems excited and leaves the office in an upbeat mood. I realize he's dealing with a lot of issues, but I'm still perplexed as to why he hasn't started his search.

He doesn't come back on Monday, and I never see him again.

This happens a lot of the time, and when I first started counseling, it was heart wrenching. I thought about it and came to some obvious conclusions. The homeless don't have the luxury of planning days the way I do. They don't carry an electronic calendar or iPad. They deal with the biggest problem they're facing at that moment. If they have a toothache, they won't do anything about it until it becomes unbearable. Every day is a struggle to find food and shelter. They may have gotten hurt and had to seek medical care. Because I don't see them again doesn't mean they blew off whatever we were working on. Maybe they just had a bigger fire to put out.

## Joshua

Today is Joshua's first full day of homelessness. He was evicted from his apartment yesterday, and robbed last night while walking the streets. They stole his bicycle, his identification, a backpack full of his clothes, and a box that contained everything else he owned. Originally from California, he moved to South Carolina a few years ago and relocated to Charlotte in the last six months. The stolen ID is registered in South Carolina. He had a North Carolina Driver's license at one time, but three years ago it was suspended for five years. He doesn't want to discuss why. Aside from that, he's extremely talkative.

His immediate need is to get into the men's shelter and catch some sleep, and he has to get there before all the beds are taken. We're near closing time at UMC, so he and I prioritize the time we have left. After a place to stay, his next priority is to get a replacement ID. We decide to complete a South Carolina affidavit for a stolen ID and get it into the mail. The replacement should arrive in three to four weeks. He plans to use the UMC address until he gets settled. He has a list of other needs including eyeglasses and prescriptions, which he can work on another day. He has a good perspective on things. He isn't moping and doesn't seem depressed or overly stressed. As he leaves the office, he thanks me and then rushes off to the men's shelter. He'll be back tomorrow to see another counselor and pick up where we left off.

## Jerry

Jerry was employed for 12 years in the recycling department in Raleigh before his license was suspended and he was fired because he couldn't drive a city vehicle anymore. Out of curiosity I ask why his license was suspended, but he doesn't want to discuss it. He's in Charlotte because he has family here, yet he's living at the men's shelter, which he's anxious to get out of. Today he applied online for two different jobs.

"Would you look at my application and let me know what you think?" He's honest about a previous arrest record, a misdemeanor 12 years ago for drunk and disorderly conduct. This may be a clue as to why he lost his license in Raleigh; he seems too eager to discuss the old arrest rather than the recent one. I advise him not to divulge the details during an interview, especially the drinking part and, if asked, to just report the charge. We role-play an interview to help him get comfortable with questions he'll most likely have to answer. We work together on suitable answers to some of the more difficult ones. Jerry has enough going against him and just needs a chance to get on with his life and off the streets.

# Walt

This is Walt's first visit to UMC. For the past week he's been living and sleeping on the streets.

"Are you staying in a camp?"

"No, by myself. In an abandoned building near here." He doesn't want to tell me the specific spot for some reason. He was living with his girlfriend and her family before an altercation between them got him thrown out last week. Originally from Boston, he moved here three years ago for the promise of a better life and abundant job opportunities. This is the first time he's been homeless. He tried to get into the men's shelter, but they wouldn't let him in without an ID. A staff member at the shelter told him that a note from his girlfriend or family member stating he was thrown out of their house and living on the streets would be enough to get him into the shelter, but her family refused to write a note for him.

I couldn't understand why the shelter didn't send him here. We normally write verification letters to the men's shelter advising them we're working with an individual and requesting they assist in any way they can. I give him a letter to get him into the shelter for the evening. In order for Walt to get a new ID, he'll need to get some documentation. I advise him to request a sealed copy of his medical records from Carolinas Medical Center (CMC). I give him a form letter that asks the medical provider to mail them to the patient using the UMC address.

He used to work at Starbucks. I ask him to call them and get a copy of one of his pay stubs with his Social Security number. He can use that to get a Social Security printout. Both of these documents will help him get a NC ID. Because it's late, I advise him to first go to the men's shelter and secure a bed for the evening. He'll be fed and able to shower and start on the ID tomorrow. He grabs my hand, pumps it up and down, and thanks me before leaving for the shelter.

# Harry

Harry recently landed a job with a landscaping company. He loves his work. He'll get paid every two weeks, and until his first paycheck, he'll need bus passes to get back and forth to the job site. He's been living in the shelter for a while and is anxious to get into a place of his own. It will be at least a month before he can afford it. His love of what he does and strong desire to be away from shelter life makes me believe this small investment will pay off. After I give him the passes, we chitchat.

"Where'd you get your enthusiasm for landscaping?"

"My mom was the biggest influence. She loved to plant things, and she was good at it. She taught me about planting and growing things and also to follow through. Man, if I messed up and didn't finish something, she'd give me a tap upside my head." His face lights up while describing her.

"Is she still alive?"

The smile vanishes. "She passed a few years ago."

"She must have been very special." His smile returns.

As I sit there, I recall something I read years ago about a mother being the single most important person in the development of a child's desire to learn and the key determinant of scholastic success.

Besides being an interesting person, Harry has a passion for what he does, and I believe him capable of one day owning his own landscape business. I wish him well as we stand together and reach out to shake hands.

## Hank

Hank just got a job at a local restaurant as a cashier. He's extremely excited at the prospect and potential for his future. He's making only about $17,000 per year but gets some benefits and opportunity for promotion. This is the chance Hank wanted, and he plans to make the best of it. He stays at the shelter and needs transportation to get back and forth to the restaurant and shelter until payday. I gave him enough bus passes to do that.

"I'm looking forward to gittin' out of the shelter as soon as I can."

"Good luck," I say as he leaves.

## Ryan

When I meet Ryan and review his past visits, I assume he's here for a food voucher. That's what he requested last time, and there's generally a pattern.

I'm mistaken. He wants to talk about a deep emotional problem he's struggling with.

He's 38 years old and works as a bartender. His income isn't predictable. For instance, this week he'll make $100 and next week he may make $250. "This time of the year is slow for the restaurant business, and my hours are generally cut back. I'll bet you don't know the staff turnover for this type of business is over 200 percent annually." He's right, I had no idea. He's homeless and has been staying with different friends or in camps. He doesn't want to stay at the men's shelter. "For a while I was staying at a band hall."

"Band hall?"

"A place bands can rent out to practice without bothering anyone."

"What instrument do you play?"

"Lots of them. I was practicing with this group. The owner didn't mind if people stayed there overnight as long as they didn't trash it out or move in with all their stuff. There's a place to sleep and a toilet but no shower. One of the guys rented a two-bedroom duplex and was looking for a roommate. We hit it off, so what the hell. Everything was working out great—and then he crashes his motorcycle. He wouldn't go to a hospital, but he was hurting so bad I made him go. I joined him."

"You're a good friend. Is he all right now?"

"When the hospital found out he didn't have

insurance, they just gave him some pain pills and sent him home. The pain was so bad he took all of them the first night, and when I came home early a couple of days later, I caught him smoking heroin."

"Go on."

Ryan looked out the window and shook his head. "Things spiraled out of control. He got addicted and was constantly scrounging for money. I had to move out. I been staying with friends or in camps."

Ryan's father lives nearby and rents a room on the outskirts of town, but Ryan won't ask to stay with him. His parents divorced when he was seven, and his father's job forced him to move to another city. "The separation hit me real hard. I turned into a hood at school."

There seems to be a common thread to his stories. He needs predictability much more than the average person. His job is unpredictable, his housing and living situation is unpredictable, and contact with his parents is unpredictable. He said, "At one time I lost contact with my father for two years." He only talks with his mother three or four times a year, primarily on major holidays. His father recently accepted a job in Boulder, Colorado, and will move away again.

Ryan begins to cry. "I'm worried about my father being there alone. He's frail and in poor health, I could lose him for good."

I give him some tissues and paper towels. "Have you ever sought professional help?"

He waves a hand dismissively. "When I was younger but it didn't work."

I urge him to consider talking with one of our social workers. He agrees, and I immediately call for one. When she comes into the room, Ryan repeats the story. She suggests he either see the social worker at the men's shelter who can refer him to a doctor, or go to Billingsley, a behavioral health center. She knows the staff at both places and offers to call and refer him.

He takes a deep breath and lets it out. "I'll decide tonight and call you in the morning."

By now he's been with me for one and a half hours and it's time to close the center. He plans to stay in a camp tonight and get some rest. "I feel safer there than at the shelter, no one will bother me."

"Come back Wednesday. I'll help you with a job search."

On the way home, I'm not feeling good about the situation and unsure if he can move forward. He doesn't come back Wednesday.

## Ellen and Ronnie

They're neatly dressed, hair combed and could pass as two school teachers. "Hi, my name is Steve" and I extend my hand and shake each of theirs. They introduce themselves as Ellen and Ronnie. "Let's go upstairs where we can talk" and I direct them to the stairs. When we reach the room I learn neither has been here before. "We'll need to get your names into the system" I explain and they both nod their heads as if expecting some formal entry process.

"I'm from St. Louis" Ellen says, "and I came here looking for work. I've known Ronnie for a while and she invited me to stay with her until I found a job."

Ronnie starts by saying "I lived in a boarding house but lost my job not long after I invited Ellen here. We both were able to get into the women's shelter run by the church on Central Ave. "

I wasn't aware of this shelter and asked how many beds they have.

"It's small with 24 beds but a third of them aren't even being used" Ellen says. "They don't seem like they care to fill em either. We got thrown out two days ago for bein five minutes late coming back to the shelter. We was interviewin for a job and we had to get back to the shelter on the bus. Five minutes is all we was late and they threw us out. They been doin that and that's why they have empty beds."

"Who runs the shelter? " I asked.

"The Salvation Army supports it but they don't run it" Ronnie says. "It run by the pastor of the church and he the one that set the rules" she says. "It like they don't care or want to listen to any excuses. We was lookin for work and couldn't get back before the curfew, but we was only five minute late" she says again, only this time an octave or two higher than the last time.

"Did you try to get into the Salvation Army women's shelter on Spratt Street?" I asked.

"They won't let us in there cause the church shelter is part of their group. We tried to get in but they say we have to wait 60 days because we was late getting back to the church shelter. We need a place to stay", Ellen says in a desperate tone of voice.

"Where did you stay last night?" I ask.

"We stay outside by the park", Ronnie says. "We can't do that anymore. We won't be able to get jobs and it just ain't safe," she says in the same desperate tone of voice as Ellen.

"How about I call the Salvation Army shelter and explain the situation as a representative of the Urban Ministry," I ask. I know sometimes a call from another agency can open a door. I also know the rule they're referring to, and the Women's shelter has a history of sticking to it. These two don't have another option for housing. There aren't other women's shelters in the city and sleeping outside, in a camp or in an abandoned building for 60 days is far to dangerous for two women.

"You can try but I know they won't change" Ellen says.

"There aren't any other options, " I say to both of them.

"Don't you have some type of housing available?" Ellen asks.

"We don't have temporary housing available here. We have a complex for the chronically homeless but that's full and there's a waiting list. Neither of you qualify anyway". I explain the difference between chronically homeless and situational homeless. I sense this is a major disappoint for them. They came here thinking we would be able to house them. The desperation level rises in Ronnie's voice.

"Yes, please call and see if it makes any difference," she says.

I call the Salvation Army shelter and ask to speak to the director. She isn't available but I'm directed to the housing manager. I explain who I am, she listens to my story and says they're at capacity now. She suggests the two women come over to register anyway for the future. I thank her and hang up.

"We already been there and they say we can't stay there for 60 days. They ain't goin to let us in, they already told us," Ellen says in frustration.

"What options do you have if you can't get into their shelter?" I ask. "It doesn't appear you have any at this time." I think you need to try again and I'm willing to call again and plead your case. As I'm preparing to call the office phone rings. It's the housing manager from the shelter.

"If your two clients can get here by 5:00 we can get them into a temporary shelter tonight. They'll have to register which takes about 30 minutes. The bus to the shelter leaves at 5:45 and if they miss it they won't have a place."

"Thanks" I say. "They'll be there." I hang up and explain the situation to Ellen and Ronnie. The Women's shelter is a 5-minute walk from here. They'll have to leave now to get there in time for registration.

"Thank you for your help" Ellen says. Her tone is a little more upbeat.

"You better get going" I say and escort them out into the walkway. We shake hands and they rush off.

I sit back down and realize all I was able to do was put a temporary fix on their situation. We need more temporary housing for women in the city. We also need to cut people a break sometimes.

## Roger

Roger was working for a temp company doing spot welding and warehouse work until he was laid off. He's 32 years old and originally from Charlotte. He and I start to talk and we get into the subject of people's perception of the homeless.

"People make judgments about you without understanding your circumstances," he says. "When you're homeless, you can't always do what you want to do every day, like take a shower in the morning." He lives in a boarding house. "My dad helped me with the rent last month, but not anymore, because he's on a fixed income." Roger's confident he'll be able to land another job quickly. He doesn't want to go to the shelter. "The boarding house ain't much but it's my own place. I share a bathroom with five other guys. It ain't always easy to live close like that. Some are neat and others are just sloppy." He sprays some saliva as he accents the final word. "The place is owned by a slumlord, but I have an air conditioning window unit, which is a blessing."

"What did you come here to talk about today?"

"I need some food from Loaves and Fishes."

"Do you have a refrigerator in your room?"

"A freezer but no fridge, but that ain't no worry, I can use one of the other guys' refrigerator." Roger's completely out of food and needs to go to a food pantry today. The closest will require a change of buses. I arrange for the food pickup, give him two bus passes, and hurry him out. He thanks me as he double-times it out of the office.

# Joe

Joe is 27 years old and originally from Georgia. He lives at the shelter and is anxious to get out of there and into an apartment. He recently landed a job as a pressure washer for a small business. He was supposed to be at work today but didn't have transportation, so he came here looking for help. I call his boss, who describes Joe as someone with a lot of energy and maybe a little hyper. The boss likes Joe's work ethic and wants him to stay, but he's running a business and needs someone dependable. "If Joe can't get here tomorrow, I'll have to find someone else for the job." I assure him Joe will have transportation to and from the work site and ask him to hold the job. Joe gets his first paycheck in two weeks.

I give him two ten-way bus passes. "You're going to be responsible for your transportation to work after your first paycheck."

He nods his head. "I know. I just need some help till then." He stands, thanks me, and we shake hands.

# Lawson

Lawson arrived in Charlotte a week ago from a small town in South Carolina. Unemployed for the last nine months, he wants a job, and is highly confident his chances of getting one here are far greater than in his hometown. He stayed in a motel the first three nights, but concerned how fast he was going through what little money he had, went to the men's shelter. He couldn't stay there because he doesn't have a North Carolina ID and is considered a non-resident. The shelter is having severe capacity problems trying to house locals and uses a triage waiting period that places non-residents at the bottom of the list. Lawson stayed outside the last four nights, didn't get much sleep, and looks exhausted.

"My family doesn't know 'bout me sleepin' outside. I don't want to worry them."

He's come to UMC every day since arriving in the city. Besides getting into the shelter, he also needs a North Carolina ID in order to get a job. He's hungry, needs food, but has nowhere to store it. He has the necessary documentation to get his ID, so I give him a waiver and a bus pass to get there. I also give him a list of places that give meals to the needy.

The situation with the men's shelter troubles me, so while he's here, I call to verify it. Sure enough, it's correct, but there's an exception he isn't aware of. If he has written documentation of an eviction or of being homeless, he can be accepted into the shelter and get a bed. I almost ask why they think someone with a home would try to stay there, but I let it pass.

I handwrite a note on UMC stationery explaining his situation and relating how he has come here every day for the last week. "I'm not sure this'll work, but it's worth a try. I want you to come back Wednesday and enter the jobs program. They'll help you with a résumé and a job search online."

He's excited at the possibility of getting a bed tonight and leaves the office upbeat. I wish him well and ask him to let me know on Wednesday what happens tonight.

I never see him again.

## Herman

Herman wants to apply for an airport job he saw advertised online at the library yesterday, cleaning the inside of planes between landings and takeoffs. "The person I talked to on the phone said I had to apply in person." I give a quizzical look, which he catches, and I decide to check the firm's website on the computer. Most jobs can be applied for online and I'm not sure the response he got was correct. In fact, the posting says he can apply online.

I wonder if he made the story up about calling and if he just wants a bus pass to sell or trade, so I ask him. He denies it, and after talking with him for a few minutes, I sense he really wants a job and may have misunderstood the person he called. "Come in Wednesday and work with the jobs program volunteers. They'll help you pull your résumé together, apply online for the job, and direct you to other firms that have been hiring homeless and have job openings. By the way, do you have a felony record or use drugs?"

"No, sir, I sure don't."

Instead of waiting until Wednesday I decide to act quickly and bring him downstairs to the computer lab to apply online for the position at the airport. Unfortunately, the lab is booked and there's a waiting list. He's coming back Wednesday anyway to meet with the volunteers who staff the jobs program and use the computer lab. I give him step-by-step guidelines on how to reach the website on Wednesday. I ask where he's staying tonight.

"In the camp across the tracks." I know the camp. He's in his mid-fifties, and I'm sure sleeping outside is hard on him physically. I shake his hand and wish him the best.

## Reggie

Reggie comes across to me as very sincere and anxious to get a job. He lost his driver's license last week, came here to get a waiver, and went to the DMV yesterday for a replacement. The agreement we have with the DMV waives the $10 fee for a state ID. Reggie asked for a driver's license, which costs $20. Whomever he talked with at the DMV wouldn't waive the $20 fee, so Reggie came back for help. I initially think he has an automobile, but I learn he doesn't. "What difference does it make if you have a state ID or a driver's license? We're not going to pay the additional $10, so why don't you get your state ID now, and when you get a job, then get your license?" He knows he needs an ID to get a job. He agrees and I give him another waiver. I also suggest he come in on Wednesday and work with the volunteers from the jobs program to find a job. He isn't aware of that service and is excited about the opportunity.

"How do I get food stamps?"

I instruct him where to go and how to apply. "Do you want some food?" He's obviously hungry because he almost jumps out of his seat when I ask him. It's late, and the Loaves and Fishes centers are closed, so he'll have to wait until tomorrow. I make arrangements for a food pickup tomorrow morning. He's staying in a camp by himself and won't be able to refrigerate anything, so I suggest he request canned goods only. "Go to the men's shelter tonight and get a bed and a good meal and stay out of the woods."

He shakes his head and says he doesn't want to do that, which isn't unusual. I give him a list of other places to get some food this afternoon, all within walking distance. The food won't be great but will sustain him until tomorrow. There's something about him that makes me feel he's genuine and sincere and would be a good employee if given the chance. We shake, and he leaves the office.

## Rory

Rory struggles into the office with a large duffel bag that holds everything he owns. He starts the conversation quickly. "I want to get out of the shelter and the only way out is a job. I need help." He summarizes his work history and experience, and it's strong—former teacher's aide, football coach, and group home manager for adults with disabilities.

"How did you end up homeless and at the shelter?"

He has an interesting story. He moved to Charlotte from coastal Carolina and moved in with a woman friend who needed some help. He didn't go into detail about the type of help or if they were planning to marry, but he trusted her enough to give her full access to his savings. Soon after arriving in Charlotte, he became severely ill, went to the emergency room, and learned he had type two diabetes. He spent a few days in the hospital to recover. When released, he found his friend had left the city with her kids and his money. He has no idea where she went. Now he's looking for work and wants to know about our programs.

I explain the jobs program while pulling up the homepage for another nonprofit that works with disabled adults. We both notice a job opening for a group home manager. I download it and ask him to go downstairs where the jobs program staff will help him with his résumé and application. He's as excited as a kid at Christmas. He drags his duffle behind him as he heads downstairs, thanking me while he walks.

## Marcus

Marcus was laid off from his warehouse job about two months ago. He drove a forklift and has certifications for operating similar industrial equipment. After the layoff, he lost his apartment. With little to no savings and not wanting to sleep at the shelter, he's been staying with different friends. He knows he's on a slippery slope trying to avoid the shelter and at the same time keep his friends. I can see he's very hopeful and excited as he sits down.

"I found a job opening in Raleigh like the one I had in Charlotte. They told me to come to the warehouse to apply and interview." He seems overly encouraged as though he is a shoo-in for the job if he can get there. He asks for $100 for bus fare to Raleigh. When I tell him we don't support that type of request, he slumps down in his chair and drops his head. There isn't an agency in the city that pays for job seeker transportation to other cities for an interview.

"Have you compared the cost to other bus companies?" I ask.

He said he did, but in reality he looked at only one site where the cost was $100 roundtrip. "Let's look at other bus companies," I say. We find two express bus companies, both priced at $20 one way. We also look at Amtrak, which has a daily trip to Raleigh at close to the express bus fare. He perks up and says he'll use his own money for the train trip tomorrow. He thanks me for working with him and leaves upbeat.

This is a good example of how the right type of help at the right time can make all the difference to a homeless person. Looking at alternative transportation options is a simple enough thought, but it may make enough of a difference for Marcus to escape homelessness. Marcus isn't lazy; he just needed someone to look at his problem in a different light.

# Hermann

Hermann wants to leave the shelter for a place of his own and asks if I can help him by making some calls with him to potential landlords. I sense he isn't comfortable talking on the phone, so I agree. He has a list of boarding houses and rooms for rent that he found online. He's only considering rooms that rent for $375 per month or less, but the list is short at that price range, and those rooms are rented quickly. His unemployment income of $150 per week is even shorter.

After our third call to potential landlords and no luck, Herman says, "I need a job." One bedroom and a shared bath aren't exactly luxurious, but it beats the hell out of the shelter. I suggest he come here Wednesday to meet with the jobs volunteers and begin an active, organized approach to finding work. He agrees he needs to give job-hunting top priority but says he can't devote much time to it.

"Why not devote most of your time to getting a job?"

"Transportation's a big problem for me. I can't take a job on the other side of town that begins at the wee hours of the day. The buses don't run all night and I won't have a way to get back and forth. Then there's the shelter—I won't have a bed if I get back too late and I'll have to sleep on a mattress on the floor until someone gets up and I take their bed. Food's another problem. I'll need lunch and don't have any money for food to bring with me."

He's in a spiral of despair that paralyzes his efforts. I offer to call the shelter about a permanent bed, but he turns it down. We part with nothing accomplished, at least in my opinion. He on the other hand thanks me and seems excited.

## Ricardo

He's wearing a New York Yankees cap with his long salt-and-pepper hair sticking straight out from the sides. His jeans are worn but look comfortable and match his blue plaid flannel shirt. His gray tennis shoes look as though they fit. He's overdressed for the weather, but that's not unusual. When you're homeless and don't have a place to put your things, you wear them. He has a spot in his left eye that seems to block his vision, but he doesn't talk about an eyesight problem, and his mannerisms don't suggest he has one.

He chooses his words carefully and talks very slow, as if afraid he'll slur his words. His voice inflection is inconsistent and I detect a faint odor of liquor. On the other hand, his vocal inconsistency may be due to lack of sleep and bone weariness from living outside in a difficult environment.

He moved here from the Northeast with a job in the construction industry, bringing with him all the tools he had accumulated over a lifetime. When work ran out, he was forced to pawn everything he owned, every last tool. A family he met here befriended him, feeds him, and lets him use their shower on occasion. He won't sleep there because they have small children and he's afraid of wearing out his welcome. He stays someplace different each night, wherever he feels safe. During the Democratic National Convention, he stayed with a group of protesters for four nights in the park because he felt safe in the crowd. He wants to get into the men's shelter but needs an ID.

I give him the waiver form but feel depressed because I can't do more. He's sixty years old and wants to get a job and work another two years. I suggest he come to the jobs program on Wednesday even though I know his chances aren't good. I offer him an alternative meal list, but he has one and is using it. I shake his hand when he leaves, sit down to stare out the window, and say a prayer for him.

## Summary

The primary reason twenty-four percent of the homeless people I counseled came to see me was for help finding a job. That doesn't mean everyone else I saw wasn't, but for this group, lack of a fair paying job was the only thing separating them from a place of their own. Climbing out of homelessness is virtually impossible without a job. Many homeless job seekers also have to combat barriers such as living in shelters, limited transportation, lack of food for meal breaks, and reduced access to educational and training programs. In a competitive environment where the unemployment rate is high, homelessness can be an almost insurmountable barrier to finding a job. Compounding this problem, many homeless are qualified only for minimum-wage jobs. A person earning $7.25 an hour, 40 hours a week, 52 weeks a year will earn $15,080, which is 19 percent below the poverty threshold for a family of three. In a minimum-wage situation, work provides no escape from poverty.

The nation's financial crisis swelled the ranks of the homeless. Many of the people I met were long-term unemployed. Most were not eligible for unemployment benefits because they had been doing nonstandard work, such as day labor, independent contracting, or working for a temporary help agency. Those eligible for benefits find themselves in a precarious situation when their benefit runs out and they end up in a shelter or, worse, on the street. Very few of the people I met had any form of health insurance, which was dangerous for the neighbor and put pressure on emergency rooms at local hospitals.

When someone came in who found a job and needed assistance with transportation or food, staff and counselors celebrated. It seemed like a small victory for everyone. There weren't a lot of happy endings in this section, but there was a lot of hope.

# 2

# The Poor

*John*

I LEAN FORWARD IN MY SEAT, edging closer to John, thinking the nearer I get to him, the better I can understand what he's saying. I finally stop, pull back in my chair and, for the third time in five minutes, say, "Please repeat that." John has a severe speech impediment that causes him to mumble. After what seems like a half-hour but is probably closer to ten minutes, I understand he wants to pick up some food today from an L&F location and also needs transportation to a doctor appointment at the mental health center tomorrow morning.

Most of the transportation provided by UMC is on public buses through the area transit authority. Bus passes are the most common and expensive service requested by neighbors. The price of bus passes has risen 20 percent over the last three years, and they cost UMC well over $40,000 annually. In order to offset some of this cost, Urban Ministry has a van that runs to regular locations on Tuesday and Thursday in the morning and afternoon. It seats up to seven people and is driven by a volunteer. I recommend John take the van tomorrow morning and return here in time for lunch, which he is agreeable to.

He smells strongly of the type of smoke generated by burning brush or wood. He says he's staying with a friend, but I suspect that might be in a camp. He doesn't volunteer additional information and I don't push him. He has no income, with the exception of food stamps. When he leaves he blesses me and shakes my hand.

## Jason

Jason needs financial assistance to pay for a sinus prescription. He has been coming here for three years and is again on the verge of homelessness. We first met in 2010 when he was living at the shelter and moving frequently from place to place. Today he stays in an apartment paid for through another non-profit agency, and he is very grateful. Besides the prescription assistance, he requests a Loaves and Fishes referral. We are able to help him with both requests.

We have a lot of neighbors today, and I don't have time to learn more about his background. I wonder if he can work and continue moving up the ladder one step at a time or if he has a medical problem that limits what he can do. He's excited for this win and for his apartment and seems motivated to do more. We shake hands, and he thanks me as he leaves.

# Barbara

Barbara's husband of 10 years recently passed away from cirrhosis of the liver and left two insurance policies naming her as beneficiary. The policies were purchased within the last two years and are worth a few thousand dollars. He did not have a will. The insurance company requested his death certificate and prior medical records to check if he had a preexisting condition when he bought the policies. Barbara has his death certificate, but the hospital won't release his medical records to anyone other than the executor of his estate. Barbara can be named the executor by a county agency, but the agency charges $135 for this service and Barbara doesn't have the money. She has a monthly net income of $600, a combination of a disability check and Social Security. Her rent is $400, leaving her $200 a month to live on. I'm not sure how she manages the rest of her expenses or if she gets additional assistance from someone. I advise her to see a lawyer and offer to pay him with the insurance proceeds. We identify four nearby lawyers for her to call. She seems fine with this as a solution and is happy to have some direction and a plan as she gathers her things and leaves the office.

# Gary

Gary just landed a job with a cleaning firm. He starts Tuesday and will be working steadily for the next month. He's staying at the men's shelter and needs a bus pass to get to work for the remainder of this week until he gets paid next Monday. I ask for the name and number of his boss in order to confirm the job, which ensures the neighbor isn't trying to get a bus pass to sell on the street. I reach his boss quickly and confirm Gary's hiring and work schedule. I give him a 10-way pass and advise him of his responsibility to pay for his bus passes once he gets paid. He doesn't say so, but I surmise he makes minimum wage, which means roundtrip bus passes will cost him a half-hour's wages each day. No easy solutions, but it's a start.

## Jennifer and Jeffery

Jennifer and Jeffery are married and live on the streets. Jennifer has bronchitis, Jeffery has pneumonia, and they both cough the entire time in the office. Although they cover their mouths, I feel besieged by germs. Both were recently at the emergency room where they received prescriptions for antibiotics and now need a voucher to get them filled. They also need refills for some behavioral health meds. They complain about the 14-day supply limit and request assistance to increase it. "We constantly need refills." They also ask for a Loaves and Fishes referral. Because they don't have a means to store perishable food or cook fresh vegetables, they'll need ready-to-eat foodstuffs.

Charlotte has no shelter for married couples, and in order to be together, they stay on the streets. Last night they slept in one of the parks downtown. During the cold months, they separate to stay at different Room at the Inn facilities and meet in the morning at UMC. The triage at Room at the Inn always gives women priority over men when deciding who gets a bed and who doesn't. Jeffery is not always able to get a place and occasionally has to stay at the men's shelter. I give them the necessary vouchers for the antibiotics, three-month refills, and food.

I admire them for the love they have for each other, even if it means sleeping outside. I wish there is more we could do.

## Marie

It's late in the afternoon when Marie comes into my office. She's in her early thirties and pregnant with her fifth child. She's feeling sickly, tells me something isn't right with this pregnancy and that she made an appointment this afternoon with her doctor. She has three requests; a bus pass to get to her doctor, direction and assistance to get a state identification card, and a referral for Loaves and Fishes.

I fear because of the late hour we won't have enough time before the doctor's office closes to gather the necessary referrals and waivers for the ID and food request. She's living with her mother. I advise her to come back tomorrow for the food voucher and the school transcript voucher and take the bus pass now to get to the doctor.

Getting her ID won't be a problem. She has her birth certificate and a Social Security card. The food referral will be quick, and because of the hour, she won't be able to pick up food today anyway. She's very lively and seems full of fun. Her sister is in the other room and comes into the office to say hello. Her sister's also pregnant.

Marie agrees with my recommendation and leaves with the bus passes. She'll be able to see someone early tomorrow to resolve the rest of her needs. She thanks me as she rushes off to get to the doctor.

## Natalie

Natalie started a new job yesterday. She comes to Urban Ministry today at 1:30 and tells me she has to be at work at 2:00.

"Why didn't you come earlier in the day?"

"Me and my fiancé hitchhiked here this morning from the other side of town to get a bus pass. You can ask him, he's in the other room." I peer over and wave to him and he waves back.

I call and verify her employment with her boss who is surprised Natalie is going to be late on her second day. I explain her situation, hoping it gives her some breathing room with her boss. I give her a 10-way pass and advise her to come back for another if she doesn't get paid in time to buy one herself.

After I give her the pass, she tells me about another problem. "We're past due on our rent and need $150 immediately or we'll be evicted." I suggest she leave for work and come back tomorrow to see a counselor and ask for help in finding names and phone numbers of agencies in the area and state that may be able to help them. She says she didn't realize there were possible solutions to their predicament and then thanks me. I wish both of them well as they hurry out.

## Dorothy

Dorothy and her husband moved to Charlotte recently and have been to the Urban Ministry before. They're originally from North Carolina but lived along the East Coast most of their lives. They came to find work and both landed temporary jobs. Upon their arrival in Charlotte, they slept outside a few nights, stayed in the shelters a few times, and took advantage of Room at the Inn. Since finding temporary work, they've been able to rent a room at a local motel.

Dorothy's handbag was stolen recently, and it contained her birth certificate and her Social Security card. She needs an ID in order to get a permanent job. Fortunately, we have a copy of her Social Security printout on file. I make a copy and give her a verification letter from the center. Luck is in her corner because her sister is mailing her original marriage license to the center, which will suffice as a proof of birth document for the ID. Between the Social Security printout, verification letter and her marriage license, the DMV should accept her application. They seem to be moving in the right direction and have a chance for a breakout at some point.

# Denny

Denny, a lifelong resident of Charlotte, is here for the first time, referred by a doctor at CW Williams, a medical facility that does pro bono work for the homeless and poor. Denny lives with his sister and her family, works as a temporary laborer, and earns about $100 per week. He has high blood pressure and needs assistance to pay for a prescription. I give him a verification letter for the sliding scale program at the pharmacy, and since he doesn't have a vehicle, a bus pass to get there. He's a pleasant person and thanks me when he leaves.

Afterwards, I consider how fortunate he is to have a sister who cares enough to let him live with her family. I sense he'll be back again.

## Helen

At the age of 62, Helen is finally able to move out of the women's shelter and into an apartment. She loves her place, and the $450 disability payment she receives monthly from Social Security goes mostly to pay rent. She's on Medicare and Medicaid but doesn't have any type of gap insurance. She needs a prescription filled for three different ear and nose medications. There's a fourth prescription for a codeine-based drug that I know we can't help with. She needs three dollars per medication. UMC will give a neighbor up to $28 per year for prescriptions. I give her a verification letter to CVS and they'll bill us the $9 directly. I advise her she's still eligible for $19 dollars more in prescription drug assistance from UMC for the remainder of the year. I know if she came to me needing money for these meds I'd personally find a way to get it for her. She thanks me and leaves the office for the pharmacy.

# Sandra

Sandra's 24 years old and has been living in a tent in a camp with another woman on the outskirts of the City Center for the past six months. Her young son lives with her mother in Charlotte. Her mother won't let her live there for reasons Sandra doesn't want to discuss. Her mother wants Sandra to get an apartment of her own and take her son. It sounds as though there was a falling out between Sandra and her mother.

Sandra works at a local restaurant doing odd jobs from washing dishes to cleaning tables. She rides her bike to work from camp and takes showers at the Urban Ministry. The manager of the restaurant gives her food. "I've been getting along as best I can." She plans to rent an apartment, has enough money saved for a deposit, and earns enough at the restaurant to pay the rent.

"I just found out I'm pregnant." I try to disguise my surprise, but too late. "My boyfriend sometimes stays with his friends and sometimes with me in my camp."

"Is he going to live in the apartment with you?"

"I don't know. I want him to get a job. I need help to get furniture and things for my apartment." A baby bed is at the top of her list along with a bed for her son. "I need a letter from here to go to the crisis assistance place." She's referring to a verification of homelessness letter. I check her file; she's been coming her since last October. I fill out the form letter and hand it to her. She is openly excited, leaps to her feet and hugs me. I wish her well and ask her to come back and let me know how she's doing. I never see her again.

## Juan

At 62, Juan is struggling with his first time being homeless. "I lived with my brother for a long time, but ten days ago we had a fallin' out over money. He told me to leave and I had to move into the men's shelter." Before moving out, Juan was approved for Social Security disability and will begin receiving a check for over $1800 per month. Although Juan doesn't say so, my sense is the disability income is at the root of the problem—his brother wants some of the newfound income and Juan said no. Juan feels he'll be fine and able to live alone with this money along with doing some odd jobs. He wants to get out of the shelter quickly. He already has some temp work lined up for three days and needs transportation. He asks for three bus passes, which I give him after verifying the work. He thanks me and leaves the office with a smile.

# Albert

Albert is not technically homeless but definitely poor. He was laid off from his job for a few months and was recently called back. He's in the food service industry and makes $8.50 an hour. He's been with his present company for over two years and likes his work. He's lived with his mother, who is on a fixed income, for 11 years, ever since he and his wife divorced.

He starts back to work next week and will need two 10-way bus passes to get back and forth until his first paycheck. He also asks for a food voucher for lunch makings he can pack and bring to work. He's comfortable he can stretch one week of food into two weeks. He realizes he'll be responsible for buying his own bus passes and food after his first paycheck. He won't have a lot of money left over. His bus passes will cost him $4 and his lunch will cost approximately $2.50 per day—about an hour's work each day devoted to food and transportation. "No matter" he says. "I think I can move up eventually and make more money." I like him because of his attitude and work ethic. We shake and he leaves with his head high.

## Justin

Justin is 61 years old and for the last four months has been living in a motel room. He collects unemployment but was overpaid and now some of his ongoing benefit is being docked to repay what he owes. As of yesterday he still owed $183. His unemployment checks have amounted to $30 weekly for the past two weeks. "Can't live on $30 a week," he says. I can't see how he was living on $180 a week. His rent alone is $177 per week. "I hustle and do a lot of odd jobs in order to make enough to survive."

He has a real dilemma. Because of the reduction in unemployment benefits, he can't pay his rent this week—he needs $177 tomorrow. Although technically not homeless today, he's $177 away from it. It's not odd for a homeless person to wait until the last minute to deal with a problem. I've seen it occur a few times before, and it was one of the major points Dale Mullennix, the executive director of Urban Ministry, made when I started. The homeless and near-homeless don't have the resources most people do nor are they aware of where to seek help. They can't get around easily and face other daily priorities like food and shelter.

There aren't a lot of options to get rent money quickly. I call two churches, but neither is able to help. I offer to call Crisis Assistance, but Justin says,

"My motel manager won't take payment from them." That statement doesn't make a lot of sense to me. Justin couldn't explain why, and I sensed he was just plain tired and stressed.

I show him notes from our guidebook that explain the Crisis Assistance mission. He looks down with furrowed eyebrows and back to me quickly; I realize he can't read. I call his motel and speak to someone on the front desk. The manager is gone and won't be back until morning. The clerk suggests Justin see the manager then about Crisis Assistance and, if the manager's agreeable, go to crisis assistance that afternoon to plead his case for the money. He'll need to bring a motel bill with him, which the manager can print in the morning. At best it's a long shot. I don't have other options and feel helpless. He still has the men's shelter to fall back on, but I know he doesn't like it there. He leaves and my stomach knots up.

## Carol

Carol is a ball of energy. She recently landed a job with a security company, soliciting sales of alarm systems over the phone. She's paid strictly on commission. She's excited about the opportunity and anxious to get started. She needs bus passes to get to and from her job until payday. I call her boss to verify the job, and learn he's also excited to have her on board. I give her a 10-way pass and she leaves pumped up and ready to get started on her job. Rather than making cold calls, she'll be soliciting people who have already expressed an interest in an alarm system, which will improve her odds of success.

# Sam

Some things don't add up and Sam's situation is one of them. Sam is living with his girlfriend, the mother of his two children. I'm surprised they're together because he was recently released from jail for assaulting her. Due to financial problems, they'll be evicted from their apartment tomorrow. Sam works in a warehouse approximately 35 hours per week making minimum wage, and his girlfriend works as a certified nurse assistant for different individual clients. At one time she had as many as three clients but currently serves one.

Sam asks for help with two different issues. He lost his NC ID and needs a replacement, and more importantly, he asks for direction on how to avoid eviction, which means he wants financial help with his rent. First we talk about supporting documentation he'll need for his ID, which takes little time because he has everything he needs. The eviction issue is much more difficult. There aren't many options for them. They don't have family or friends to fall back on. I suggest his girlfriend and children go to the Salvation Army emergency women's shelter today to secure beds and shelter, and he go to the men's shelter to do the same. At least they'll all have beds and food. There isn't a family shelter in town, and they'll have to live like that until they work through their financial problems and secure a new apartment. This will be a difficult transition for all of them.

He'll need to find a better paying job or one that he can work 40 hours or more per week. I suggest he come back Wednesday and meet with someone from the jobs program. They can help with his résumé and job leads. I also suspect their financial issues are complicated and involve some personal debt that can't be avoided. I give him a DMV waiver dated for Wednesday, which will give him time to get his paperwork together.

## Ruth

Ruth and her 16-year-old son sit across from me, hungry but hopeful. Their days are a struggle for enough food to subsist and they survive through the generosity of various soup kitchens in the city. She requests a Loaves and Fishes referral and informs me they're waiting for their food stamp allotment to begin. She's close to starting a minimum wage job and he'll start school soon and be eligible for meal support. They live with an elderly friend who's on a fixed income. I make arrangements for them to pick up a week's worth of food tomorrow. They're both thankful and grab my hand to shake it. How fortunate they are to have a friend who lets them stay in their home until they get on their feet.

## Sharon

Sharon has just landed a job with the *Charlotte Observer*. She moved here from Georgia and lives with her children. Because she's a rehire, she wasn't asked to show her North Carolina ID, which is a good thing for her because she doesn't have one. Getting one won't be a problem for her because she has the supporting documentation needed. All she needs from me is the fee waiver form.

Now that she's working again, she wants to get her own apartment. She inquires about rent assistance and how to go about applying for it. I refer her to Crisis Assistance, the experts in this particular area. She leaves in a good mood.

# Keiston

Keiston's a 19-year-old who moved in with his sister after living on the streets for a short time. He was born in North Carolina and attended high school in Delaware. His ID was stolen last night and he needs a replacement. He's been here before, and the last time he was here we made a copy of his Social Security card. He has a medical history in Charlotte and can get his sealed medical records at the University Hospital. I give him bus passes to the hospital and the DMV along with a DMV waiver. We shake hands, and I wish him well

# Andre

Andre just got a part-time job cleaning homes and exterminating any vermin he finds inside. He asks for a 10-way bus pass to get back and forth to work until payday. He doesn't have the phone number of his employer but says they're online. I find the number, call, and ask for the owner, who confirms he hired Andre for three or four days of work per week. Payday's every other week. After hanging up I explain to Andre the pay/transportation policy, which I sense he already knows. He's in his late 30s and

Stephen Pernotto

lives at the shelter. "I get it, I'll have to buy my own passes after payday. I just need to get there now. I'm also working on my GED and should be done in a few weeks." I congratulate him on his perseverance and say he might be able to get a better job with a GED. He says, "I had a few felonies in my past but that's all behind me now. I gotta do something to improve myself."

He tells me he's being paid cash rather than by check. Technically, he's being treated as a contractor, and this arrangement will work out better for him in the short term. He's earning a little more than minimum wage now, and I suspect his background wasn't checked through the temp agency. Long-term, it could hurt him financially. Getting a job is a big deal for the people I meet no matter what the situation. We finish, reach out to shake hands, and say good-bye. He thanks me.

## Keith

Keith is the best news of the day. He just landed a job with a construction firm laying foundations and building homes. He needs bus passes until payday. I call his boss to verify Keith's employment. The boss sounds alarmed.

64

"Is there a problem? Something I should know about? He do something wrong?"

I reassure him I'm only trying to help Keith with transportation to the job site. I hold my breath.

"That's good," the boss says. "I'm kinda counting on this guy. I think he'll fit in good with my crew. I really need him here tomorrow."

"He'll be there."

Keith's living in the shelter, and I don't think his boss realizes that. Keith plans to get into an apartment of his own when he accumulates enough for a deposit. I give him enough bus passes to get him to his first payday and wish him well.

# Summary

Twenty percent of the people I counseled were so poor they couldn't afford to pay for the basic necessities of life including food, shelter, and clothing. The income they had was below the government poverty threshold of $23,050, sometimes by as much as 50 percent. This could be categorized as extremely poor. I didn't attempt to find the root cause of poverty of the neighbors I talked with, but I did find common denominators to their predicament. In most cases, several contributing factors were in

Stephen Pernotto

play, which made it all the more difficult to break out of this cause of homelessness. For example, a single-parent household usually has less income than a two-parent household and can't afford a financial safety net to cushion it from an unplanned financial problem, such as job loss or a medical necessity. Ten of the most common attributes I saw, in no particular order:

1. Born poor. They start poor and can't break the cycle.

2. Inadequate education. They don't have the technical or life skills needed to compete in the workplace and can't get a well-paying job, even at the poverty level.

3. Substance abuse. They use their resources to support a drug or alcohol problem and become undependable to everyone around them.

4. Single-parent households. Living on a single income and missing the support of a mate.

5. Medical and mental problems. In some cases, they start out with a medical or mental problem, in others, the stress associated with being poor can lead to these problems.

6. Lack of a mentor or role model. Especially prevalent in single-parent households but

also within the community. Parents, teachers, coaches and clergy fill this role in many cases, but mostly parents.

7. Misfortune. A disaster of some sort devastates a family, which may already have been fragile due to other factors, and it can't recover.

8. Fraud and theft. Being taken advantage of and losing what little wealth they have accumulated.

9. No safety net. Living on the edge and spending beyond one's means to keep up appearances or for other reasons. A job loss or other setback causes a collapse.

10. By choice. A very small percentage are just lazy and prefer to depend on welfare and social programs.

There's no known single cause of poverty. However, the effects are serious. Children born into poverty suffer more persistent health problems than do children in better financial circumstances. Kids in poverty tend to miss school more frequently and have more medical and mental issues. Stress correlates strongly with poverty, and its effects include violence, abuse, depression, and disruption in work, school and family relationships.

In this chapter, you saw both causes and effects of being poor. I don't offer solutions because I don't have answers. My inclination is that most of the neighbors I met would benefit from a mentor or role model who could give them consistent support and direction beyond the 45 minutes a volunteer like me spends with them. We apply Band-Aids. To really make a difference, they need someone who can perform surgery.

Someone once said to me, "We can't solve world hunger, but we sure as hell can make a difference in one person's life if we devote the time and energy."

# 3

# Mental Illness

## Billy

BILLY HAS AN IDENTITY ISSUE. HE'S Mexican American, has been homeless for the last twenty years, and is the most chronically homeless person I've ever met. As a little boy, he suffered physical abuse by his father, and it's remained with him his entire life. He has an out-of-state ID, a Social Security card, and a birth certificate, and he wants a North Carolina identification card. The name on his Social Security card doesn't match the names on his birth certificate and ID as it has his middle name on it. The North Carolina DMV refused to give him an ID because of the discrepancy. This is a judgment call and could be interpreted differently in another DMV office.

He has pay stubs from the day labor pool with the last four digits of his Social Security number on them. I give him a DMV waiver letter along with two bus passes and direct him to another DMV office with his birth certificate, out-of-state ID, and pay-stubs in search of a more understanding clerk and a different decision. He plans to go Monday rather than tomorrow, Friday, when he works downtown as a panhandler because his best prospects, other Mexican Americans, are generally paid on Friday. He gives me a demonstration of how to panhandle. I have to admit, he's good.

He begins talking about the physical abuse he endured as a child in Mexico. While a baby, his father intentionally kicked him in the head, and the trauma to his brain had a lifelong impact. His learning ability shattered, he was unable to attend school and lived with his mother for 15 years before leaving home on his own. Compounding his mental health issues, he became addicted to alcohol. He lives on the street, at times in cardboard boxes, wherever he can lay his head down to sleep. He stays at a shelter occasionally when he can find an opening. His low self-esteem manifests in his exaggerated negative feelings toward himself, a constant flow of criticism. He believes he's completely alone and no one cares whether or not he's alive. He speaks often about his strong religious belief and describes himself as a Christian. He seems to be searching for some personal comfort.

I ask him to complete a vulnerability index study; possibly he could be a candidate for acceptance into a Moore's Place apartment for the chronically homeless. He agrees to this and for a moment steps out of his reality at the thought of his own place. I feel guilty, as if I misled him, knowing it won't be built for another two years. I don't care. He needs to latch on to some hope and find comfort somewhere.

## Leigh Ann

She's a severe schizophrenic and normally harmless but can be volatile and cause a scene if provoked. When I meet her downstairs, she remembers me from a year ago and gives me a hug and a kiss on the cheek. She's well known to the staff and other volunteers. As we walk the stairs she tell me she's sick and will explain it all when we get to the office. We sit down.

"I'm not feeling well and spittin' up a lot of somethin' green." I'm glad lunch isn't anytime soon as she continues describing her ailment. I don't ask for more information, fearing she'll give it to me. She called the doctor's office, and they request she come in immediately. She has become skilled at manipulating. Very possibly she's lying, but I take her at her word and give her two bus passes to get to the doctor's office immediately. She thanks me and rushes off.

## Dave

At an early age, Dave watched his father murder his mother and managed to get away when his father tried to kill him. He's 57, walks with a crutch, and has an irreversible condition in his leg that causes his arteries to harden, which severely limits his mobility.

He has regular doctor appointments coming up, and I give him bus passes for the two this week. He starts talking about his past and the life journey that brought him here today. He lives in the men's shelter. He grew up in a foster home, has attempted suicide twice, and has a history of cutting himself, which he swears he hasn't done in a while. He suffers from depression and is taking medication to manage it. A former crack addict but clean for the last eight years, he grew up on the West Coast and came to Charlotte for a better chance of landing a job. It didn't work out, and he's now homeless. Short, concise, rather matter of fact, but it's his story as he tells it. He wants to have his leg treated, his disabilities approved by the SSA, and get a place of his own. He seems frail and fragile, capable of breaking up at any moment and splitting into a hundred pieces.

He likes to read, and I suspect he uses books as a means of escape from the reality of his life. He's reading *The Purpose Driven Life* and finding great comfort in it. He seems to be searching for some personal peace.

# Charles

Charles thinks someone is going to kill him today. He looks groggy, his eyes darkened and his lids in a soft droop from too little sleep at the shelter. "Has anyone threatened you or indicated in some way they are going to kill you?" I ask in a soft slow voice. He shakes his head slowly. He looks down at his hands and watches his fingers move in a rote pattern on the back of his wrist. "Has anyone ever tried to kill you before?" Again, he shakes his head, shoulder to shoulder. "Why do you think someone will try today?"

"I don't know, I have a feeling."

Between snippets of conversation, I scan his report for some direction. I'm concerned because he has previously shown suicidal tendencies and signed a no-harm agreement, which is in his folder. A no-harm agreement is a contract with yourself to be mindful of your value and not to intentionally harm yourself. I want to know how he's feeling at present and ask questions about the weather, his family, and his hometown, looking for some spark of interest. There's very little reaction. He draws a pattern on the back of his left hand with a straightened paper clip and keeps his eyes cast downward to the floor. "What do you want to talk about?"

"I have to get to a doctor's appointment tomorrow and need a bus ride. Here's the card." He hands me an appointment card from the mental health clinic with his doctor's name and number. Internally I breathe a slight sigh of relief because he'll see a medical professional. I give him two bus passes.

Bus passes in hand, he seems to loosen up a little. He tells me there's a history of depression in his family. He's begun taking medication, but it hasn't affected his behavior yet. I ask if he wants to sleep in a vacant office until closing time, and he says no. There are long moments of silence between us, and I wonder if I should bring him to the clinic today. He doesn't seem suicidal during our time together, but his history and conversation concern me. He stands up and says he's ready to leave. He seems okay, so I decide to let him leave instead of trying to bring him to the clinic. "Come back whenever you want to talk."

I wonder if I'm enough help for him today or whether I'll hear some bad news tomorrow.

# Ronald

Ronald seems confused, depressed, and tired. He's rambled on for 10 minutes without a point or clear topic before I interrupt and ask why he's here. He reaches into his pants packet, pulls out a neatly folded piece of paper, and hands it to me to read. After reading the two-paragraph note, I don't know any more about him than I did when he first came in. The paragraphs lack any coherent thought and are best described as gibberish. He requests I place it in his folder. In my opinion, Ronald needs to see a mental health professional; he also needs some sleep. I lean forward in my chair and ask where he stayed last night. His answer doesn't surprise me: "In a park." I ask if he has plans for this evening, and he doesn't.

He can't stay on the streets tonight in his present condition. "When you leave this office, I want you to get into the line to stay at one of the Room at the Inn churches tonight." I ask him to come back tomorrow morning to see the nurse for a referral to a doctor at the mental health center.

When he leaves my office, I walk downstairs to talk with the coordinator for Room at the Inn program. I ask her to place him high on the triage list. She knows him and informs me that Ronald caused a commotion the previous evening at a church, and she's concerned about placing him into a situation where people don't know how to deal with him if he acts up again. I give her my opinion on his personal state of mind and how he needs help tonight as well as tomorrow. She promises to help and suggests I also discuss his situation with the social worker on duty.

The social worker knows Ronald but she's also at a loss as to how to help him. He has a record of taking medication for mental illness, showing some signs of improvement, then quits taking it. He's on my mind at the end of the day and into the evening. I don't know what to do besides what I already did, and I know it isn't enough.

# Linda

Homeless for the last five years, Linda is a young mother with an 8-month-old baby. She stays at the women's shelter. She and the baby came here today because she needs an identification card to get a job.

I ask if she has job prospects. She shakes her head and says she can't get a job until she gets her ID and won't start looking until then. A native Charlottean, Linda's formal schooling ended with tenth grade.

Sitting across from me with the baby carriage wedged in next to her between the door and my chair, she's anxious to share her background. She's a crack addict, enrolled in a substance abuse program for three days through the women's shelter. I wonder if this if her first time in such a program and how committed she is to beating her addiction. Later I wish I would have been less cynical and asked her that question. She also suffers from depression, does not take her medication regularly, and frequently falls into deep depressive moods.

Her baby, on the other hand, is a bundle of joy and happiness. She lights up the dull office with her laugh and smile, unaware of the situation her mother and she are in. I wonder if the baby will fall victim to some of the consequences associated with her mother's addiction; time will tell. As Linda talks, I can't help but notice her facial formation isn't balanced. She looks as though she had been hit hard on the left side of her face and her bones had never healed properly. Her mouth and jawbone are skewed to the right side of her face. Her left cheek has a deep depression and her mouth contorts when she speaks so that her words flow from the right side of her mouth.

I try not to gawk; it may be a birth deformity. I don't ask.

Linda has the necessary documentation to get an ID, and we complete the waiver form. I ask her to come back Thursday to get lunch for her and her daughter and a ride in the van to the DMV for her ID. She agrees to this and assures me she will be here. As she leaves, I pray for her baby's sake that she can find the right life path.

## Matthew

A 25-year-old man from the Midwest, Matthew has been homeless for three years, living between the street and the men's shelter. He slept on a downtown park bench last night and now looks extremely groggy and tired. He suffers from a host of mental health issues including schizophrenia, paranoia, depression, and bipolar disorder. He needs rides to the behavioral health center for an appointment and to a temporary job site tomorrow. I ask if he is taking his meds.

He hesitates then half nods. "Sometimes. They make me gain weight. I don't want to get fat and out of shape."

"Why does that matter if you're living in the streets?"

As a teen, he boxed in the golden gloves and he still dreams of boxing again.

"Are you training?" I ask.

He stares at me for a few moment then shakes his head. "Not yet."

He qualifies as a chronically homeless person who will need assistance to get out of the spiral, but our resources are limited and Moore's Place is full with a waiting list. I give him enough bus passes to get to his appointments and wish him well. I wish there was more we could do.

# Timothy

Timothy, recently released from an 80-day jail term, has severe behavioral issues including schizophrenia and depression, and takes medication every day to manage them. He also has a substance abuse problem, specifically with cocaine. While in jail he was interviewed and assessed for admission to a transitional housing program operated by a nonprofit organization whose mission is to assist and help cultivate a smooth transition from jail to the general population for former substance abusers. Timothy has an assigned coordinator from the agency who worked with and counseled him in preparation for his release. Because it was Easter week, Timothy was released earlier than planned without the knowledge of his counselor or the agency, and with only three days of medication. Around Easter, many people, including his counselor and the agency staff, took time off work, so Timothy went to the men's shelter, anticipating a short stay until he reached his coordinator.

Now, twelve days later and still unable to reach anyone at the agency, his medication is wearing off and he's becoming more and more confused. He doesn't have money or a cell phone and makes calls from the men's shelter and the Urban Ministry. When I meet him downstairs, he is definitely on edge. He explains his situation clearly, but there's a sense of panic in his voice and manner. He says whomever he talks with on calls to the agency is unable to confirm his admission to the program or find his records.

None of this adds up for me so I call the agency, talk to a supervisor, and learn Timothy has indeed been accepted into the program. His coordinator returned today after being on vacation. The supervisor I'm talking with informs me there's a psychiatrist on staff who can see Timothy tomorrow and give him a prescription for his behavioral medication. She also gives me the phone number of his coordinator.

The coordinator's phone mailbox is full but fortunately the coordinator and psychiatrist are in the same office building. I give Timothy a roundtrip bus pass to the agency office tomorrow to see the psychiatrist and his coordinator. I also give him my phone number in case there's a problem. He thanks me, but I can still see the panic in his eyes.

I don't hear from him the next day and hope he made it.

# Larry

Larry, a native Charlottean with a history of mental illness and homeless for the last five years, lives under the I-277 overpass not far from our building. He's excited because he found temporary work and will earn a few dollars for the next several weeks. He has to get to and from the job site and will need a 10-ride bus pass until his first payday. I call the temporary agency, confirm the job, and give him the pass. I wonder how many temp jobs turn into full-time employment and hope this is one of them. We shake hands and he rushes out of the office.

# Elizabeth

Elizabeth suffers from bipolar disorder and depression. She stays at the women's shelter and comes to the Urban Ministry to shower, seek counseling, and eat. She wants a bus pass to the mental health clinic to see her doctor and get a new prescription. I suggest she take the van tomorrow morning, but she says she has another appointment tomorrow and really wants to see the doctor today.

As a regular, she understands the processes. Her eyes avoid mine, she looks down when she talks about tomorrow's appointment, and her tone of voice makes me suspect she plans to sell the bus pass. I probe but am unable to confirm my suspicions. I can't verify today's appointment because she doesn't have one and says she plans a walk-in visit. I give her roundtrip bus passes and she thanks me.

Who am I to judge this? Dale said something to me when I first started counseling. "If you're going to err, err on the side of compassion." I tell myself I was compassionate.

## Michelle

Michelle and her young son have been homeless for more than three years. She's had to learn to manage her mental health issues, including some frightening phobias she's had all her life. She's bipolar, suffers from depression, and is taking medication for both. She's afraid of tight, enclosed areas and can't get into elevators or stay in cars for any length of time.

She came today because of a pulled muscle in her lower back, which is causing a lot of pain. She barely made it upstairs to the office and wants to go to the hospital today for treatment. She also asks for food for herself and her son.

I notice a deep scar across her left cheek, which looks as though she was hit hard at some point in her life. I brush my hand across my own cheek. "What happened?"

"Traffic accident a few years ago, I got cut up real bad. Never healed right." I sense her self-consciousness and drop the subject. I give her a bus pass to the hospital today and arrange for her to pick up food tomorrow from a Loaves and Fishes distribution point.

She's optimistic about a few things. She recently began a search for housing through another agency and believes she's close to approval. She's upbeat throughout our discussion and I wish her well as she leaves.

## Diane

Diane needs a ride to the mental health facility tomorrow for an appointment and to pick up a prescription. Our van runs there tomorrow and she'll be able to catch it early enough to make her appointment and get back here for lunch. She's living on the streets after having been thrown out of the women's shelter last week. She must have done something wrong to have that happen but denies any knowledge of it. She slept in the Fourth Ward Park last night.

She has a college degree from a West Coast college. She arrived here earlier this year, lived with friends before a falling-out, and then moved into the women's shelter. There she heard about a program in South Carolina that offers transitional housing for women with mental health issues and is anxious to learn more about it and move there. We look online for the program and discover a number of transitional housing options for women in that state.

"Why don't you try to find something here?" I ask.

"I don't like it here. I want to get out of Charlotte." I point out that South Carolina has residency requirements. "I don't care, I'll live there and become a resident if I have to."

I print a copy of the entire list with phone numbers. She has a particular interest in one of them and seems genuinely optimistic about the prospect, but I'm not sure how she intends to follow through with it. I suggest she use the phone bank and start calling all of the facilities on the list to learn more and compare them. She's excited now and thanks me for helping her. She needs a place to live, and I hope this works for her. We shake hands, and she leaves for the phone bank down the hall.

# Chris

Chris is completely delusional. He starts off by saying, "I just won a lawsuit against the state for eleven million dollars due to unlawful imprisonment."

I raise my eyebrows. "Then what are you doing here?"

"I couldn't get my money released because I was still in prison when I won the case."

"Were there two different sentences?"

"No just one." I lean back in my chair and he quickly starts on another subject. "I write songs. You probably heard some of them." He names three songs I know he didn't write. "Know what nationality I am?" He's clearly African American. "Italian and German. Billy Graham's a cousin of mine and in the distant past Lucky Luciano is an uncle of some kind."

I don't know what to say. He continues on, describing different types of trusts he has to protect his investments. "I want a bank account in order to electronically transfer my eleven mil, but I don't have twenty bucks to open it." At this point I think he might be here to get money from someone who will believe his story.

All in all, it's an entertaining 30 minutes, but I have to get back to work. I suggest he come back on Thursday to meet with a pro bono attorney. "Good idea," he says. When he leaves, I wonder if I should have suggested he see a doctor at Billingsley. I don't think we'll see him again.

# Latanya

There's an edge about her that usually means immediacy to the visit. I quickly learn I'm right and her situation is complicated. She relocated here from Ohio two weeks ago and rented a room in a home owned by a family. Within three days of moving in, she was arrested, thrown out of the home, and living on the streets. She spent the last two days in the women's shelter but can't stay there any longer.

She was asked to leave the shelter due to their local residency restriction rather than something she did. She's looking for a place to stay, and if she doesn't find one, she'll sleep outside tonight. While she was waiting to see a counselor, one of the neighbors told her there are a number of housing options available and the counselor should be able to tell her about them. She's here to explore those options.

"Why were you arrested?"

The arrest was for an assault on the son of the family. As she explains the story to me, the circumstances and reasons she hit him keep changing. It sounds as though she may be making up parts of the story as she goes along, and she and the son have similar behavioral issues. She gets disability income for mental illness. More than once during our discussion, she tests my patience. She gets angry quickly and flares up if things don't go her way. I stoke her anger by telling her there aren't many, if any, options for housing tonight.

"I was told there are lots of them. Do you know what you're doing?"

"Not usually." The levity doesn't work with her.

I decide the best thing to do is call the women's shelter on her behalf. They tell me the same thing they told her: they only accept county residents, and because she doesn't have an ID and has been here less than 30 days, she can't stay there. Their resources are extremely limited. I suggest she try the battered women's shelter and make up a story about being abused. She calls the battered women's shelter with me in the room and makes up a story involving the son of the family she was staying with, describing the two of them as former intimate partners and herself as a victim of his violent nature. It's all to no avail. They don't have room either. She gets frustrated with me and asks to see a specific staff person who was recommended by a neighbor she met downstairs. The staff person is in a review session with another neighbor and won't be available for another 45 minutes.

I suggest she get her NC ID tomorrow and I give her a waiver. As for tonight, I have to tell her honestly I don't have an answer, and she can wait downstairs for the staff person to become available. She leaves frustrated and fearful. I walk to another counselor's office and discuss the situation with her. She saw three women today who were also looking for a place to stay but will have to sleep outside tonight. I feel helpless.

## Fred

As he walks up to me from the waiting area, I can't help but notice how neatly he's dressed. He's wearing a pressed pair of khaki pants with a blue Nautica jacket, a black designer logo baseball cap, and brown athletic shoes. Ear buds attached to a cord dangle on each side of his shoulder. His hand reaches out. "I'm Fred," he says in a very soft voice.

As we walk up the steps, I ask how it's going.

"Not good."

"Where you staying?"

"The shelter."

In the office, I ask for the last four digits of his Social Security number to pull up his file. Nothing is there so I begin the process of entering him into the system. "Relax, this won't take long."

He slouches and sighs. "Time's the one thing I got plenty of."

I learn he's in his mid-fifties and separated. When I complete the data entry, I lean forward in my chair and ask what he wants to talk about.

"In December, something snapped in my head and I had to admit myself to the mental hospital. I don't know what happened, but I ended up on the floor curled up in a ball and screaming. I thought someone was going to shoot me."

"Was that the first time this happened?"

He explains that throughout his life he's had small bouts of depression and anxiety, but they were minor compared to this and he was able to manage them. I ask if he was prescribed any medication.

"An antidepressant and some anxiety pills. The anxiety is a little better, and I still get deep depressive moods." He tears up and wipes his eyes. "This is one of the things that happen when I get depressed. I can't stop it." He explains he has episodes of anger once or twice a week. He imagines he's cramped up in a box, hiding from someone who wants to shoot him. Depression always follows these episodes. "I'm reaching out for some help. I want to get my life back." He and his wife separated a week ago and he had to move into the shelter. He goes on to tell me how he worked as a skilled craftsman for twenty-five years before this happened. "I want my life back," he says a second time. "I need to stay someplace that can help me balance this medicine until it works right."

I wonder if he's suicidal right now and ask him outright. "I don't want to kill myself now…but I'm worried I might end up there"

I consult our reference book and find an agency that deals with mental health assessments and can lead to various outcomes including outpatient or residential treatment. I call and reach someone who identifies himself as Paul. I explain the situation. Paul sounds concerned and wants to help. He asks if the client is there with me. "Can I talk with him?" I hand Fred the phone.

Fred explains his situation again to Paul and is on the phone for 25 minutes. They arrange an appointment for an assessment tomorrow morning and hang up. I ask Fred how he feels, and he says his mood is starting to get better.

"It comes up when I least expect it and then goes away. I hope they understand that tomorrow." I try to reassure him and ask if he has transportation to the assessment center tomorrow. "No, I don't." I give him two bus passes and he thanks me. He stands up and reaches out to shake my hand again. "I took up a lot of your time and I'm sorry for that." I thank him for sharing everything with me and ask him if he feels ready to leave the office. "I'm okay now," he says and leaves. I pray he gets what he needs tomorrow.

# Summary

Fourteen percent of the people I met suffered from some form of mental illness that I deemed severe enough to be the primary reason for their homelessness. Serious mental illness disrupts people's ability to carry out essential daily tasks and to form and maintain stable relationships. It causes people to misinterpret others' actions towards them and to react irrationally. It often pushes away family, friends, and those trying to help and who, in many cases, are the reason they aren't yet homeless. Homeless neighbors with mental illness also run the risk of poor health habits. They can't take care of themselves and neglect precautions against disease. Additionally, many suffer from some form of substance abuse. All of this makes it extremely difficult to obtain employment and residential stability.

The Urban Ministry, with the leadership of many dedicated and talented individuals from throughout the community, developed Moore Place, which opened in 2012. Moore Place is Charlotte's first permanent supportive housing complex for the chronically homeless. It consists of 85 units to house individuals who were previously destitute. Most of the inhabitants are suffering from some form of mental illness or disability and have been homeless for years.

Moore Place isn't a new idea. It follows a model for housing that was already implemented successfully in cities such as New York, Portland, Denver, Salt Lake City and Richmond. The economic benefits are significant, with an average daily cost of $29.50 per person, compared to a night in jail for $150 or a visit to the emergency room at $1029. There is a great need for many more facilities like this, but it will take time and a lot more money. Moore Place has programs and services that include treatment and assistance to reintegrate back into the community. The odds of recovering from mental illness on the streets is almost nil. Moore Place and other housing solutions like it give people a fighting chance.

There is some good news about the chronically homeless, both nationally and locally. Their numbers are decreasing, down 19 percent from 2007 to 2012. In Charlotte, the number of chronically homeless decreased by 17 percent from 2010 to 2012. Due to a lack of consistent data, local trends are difficult to identify. This number was derived from the vulnerability index, used to identify the chronically homeless at the Urban Ministry.

This chapter's stories include tales of abuse, murder, irrationality, addiction, and delusion. Most of the neighbors profiled are chronically homeless and stand little chance of breaking the cycle without some form of outside intervention. Some are reaching out for help with a strong desire to stabilize their emotional swings and do whatever is needed to get back on track. They're good people trying to survive as best they can on the streets.

# 4

# Prison

## Thomas

HE IS IN A SUIT AND looks out of place in the waiting area where the normal attire is jeans and T-shirt. He has a spritely step as he walks toward me and radiates confidence. I guess he's in his mid-thirties and wonder why he's here.

When we reach the office he starts talking immediately. Thomas has spent 14 years of his life in prison, a little less than half of his waking days. The last four years in prison were for drug convictions, specifically for selling cocaine. Upon his recent release he moved back home to Charlotte where he hopes to turn his life around. He says he's living with family but doesn't define the relationship beyond that. He's dressed in a suit today because he has a job interview.

I'm impressed how polite and respectful he is. He applied for food stamps at the Department of Social Services this morning and was told they needed a copy of his conviction record in 2008 and 2009 before he could be approved. I assume someone is driving him from place to place but don't ask. Most agencies charge a fee for copies of records, and since he has no money, we spend 30 minutes online trying to get them for free. I am more hopeful than confident about it, but fortunately, we find the county site of his conviction, and his records are available online at no charge. As his records begin to print out, we're both surprised at the length of the report.

"I'm embarrassed you have to see that," he says as the printer spits out page after page. I think this may be the first time he has confronted it in its entirety. "Now you probably think I'm a bad person, but I changed, I really changed this time. I don't want to go back there again." He won't discuss the other ten years of his incarceration but only says it was not drug related. He leaves with the documents to complete his food stamp application, along with the answers to a number of unanswered questions I have. I wish him well.

# *Reggie*

He's wearing work boots with a thick ring of mud caked around the soles and splashed upwards onto the sides. A white hardhat tied to a backpack flops back and forth against his leg as he walks. He's tall, and his arms are muscular and hard. His warm smile puts me at ease as he stretches his hand out to shake mine. A bandana covers the top of his head to protect his hair. As we walk up the steps to the office I ask how he's doing.

"Better, I have a job."

"In construction?" He smiles at my little joke. His name is Reggie and he just started this job. He lives at the shelter for now and is anxious to get out.

"Nothin' but a bunch of no-goods and thieves there. Can't trust anyone with anything, and no one wants to give the next guy a break. Lousy attitudes and lots of drugs. Great place to start over, you think?"

He knows he's lucky to have this job. He spent the last eight years of his life in prison and was released just three months ago. Not many employers hire felons so quickly. He doesn't say so, but he most likely landed this job through a temp agency. He needs bus passes to get him to payday. I give him a 10-way and ask casually where he did his time.

"A bunch of different prisons, 'bout thirteen total." He goes on to explain the reward system for prisoners with good behavior. They can earn points that bring different levels of rewards and additional freedoms. "Working outside, better food, more freedom within the prison walls, and suchlike." Points are earned for consistently good behavior and result in transfers to better prisons within the system. He's glad to be free and wants to do whatever it takes to support himself on the outside. I wonder what he did to get sent to prison, but I don't want to be nosy. I shake his hand and wish him well, and he thanks me before leaving.

## Laura

She looks out of place here. Dressed in a pink sweat suit with matching pink tennis shoes, she seems to belong at a grocery store shopping for her family's dinner. Before she arrives at the front desk, I'm told she just finished an eight-month prison sentence. She smiles as I introduce myself and shakes my hand warmly; I notice she has no teeth. We walk up the flight of stairs to the office, where I begin to input her data into the system. I ask where she's living.

"I just left prison after bein' there for eight months." She was sentenced on a drug-related charge and is staying at a halfway house. Originally from the West Coast, she tells me how her sister died unexpectedly two years ago, and her life spun out of control. She describes in broad strokes how she started drinking and taking drugs, developed an addiction, and eventually ended up in prison. Other bits and pieces come out during our conversation but not in chronological order. She was also charged with abuse of an elderly person, but after bringing it up, she declares her innocence and moves the conversation along.

"I need a North Carolina ID to open a bank account to pay my bills and have my Social Security check deposited." This shouldn't be a problem since she has her prison ID and a Social Security printout. I complete the necessary forms and ask if there's anything else she wants to talk about today. She says she decided to come to Charlotte because of a book she read that used the city as a backdrop, and she asked to be placed here in a halfway house after her release. She attends regular meetings for her addictions and feels she's on the right path. She whispers softly, "I'm HIV positive and taking a cocktail mixture to manage it." She describes other medications she's on to deal with depression and bipolar disorder.

"I need to find a payee to help me manage my money and pay my bills. I can't do it by myself." We look online and find a nonprofit bill payer program she can look into. As we talk, I realize she gets confused easily and has trouble prioritizing tasks. I write down each task she needs to complete, in chronological order. I give her a bus pass to get back to the halfway house.

As she walks away, I think about how I originally felt she looked out of place, yet she's dealing with similar issues many of the neighbors have. How deceiving initial appearances can be.

# Anthony

After his release from a county work farm last week, Anthony moved into a halfway house owned and operated by a friend of his. He's married, 49 years old, and a certified electrician looking for steady work. His wife lived with her mother while he was incarcerated. His life began to unravel three years ago when he was arrested on a DUI charge. Placed on probation for this offense, he broke it nine months later for a similar offense. His driver's license was suspended this time, and he was sent to prison because it was his second DUI offense.

He's here for help to secure a North Carolina ID and for bus passes to get back and forth to a temp agency while he looks for work. We complete the waiver form and check to ensure he has the proper documents to get his ID. I can't help him with the bus passes because he doesn't have a job.

"I'm embarrassed to be askin' for this type of help, but I swear I learned my lesson this time and I don't drink anymore." He needs an apartment for him and his wife because her mother said his wife must leave after he's released from the halfway house. He has six months there, which seems to be plenty of time.

"Stay clean and away from the booze," I tell him.

We shake hands. "This time is for real," he says, "I'm telling you." I discreetly sniff the air but don't smell any liquor. He leaves the office, and I'm quietly hopeful.

## Jose

Jose has been homeless off and on for the last ten years. He struggles with alcoholism, substance abuse and mental health issues. He moved here from the West Coast after serving a felony sentence and lives in a camp with three others. He talks about his living conditions and why he chooses to live in a camp rather than a shelter. "It's less stressful and more peaceful in a camp, I can come and go as I please and have two friends in the camp with me." He showers at the Urban Ministry, and because the camp is near a small creek, he can wash and brush his teeth regularly. Sometimes he goes to bed hungry, but most often he finds food.

He needs behavioral health meds and came to the Urban Ministry today for a prescription voucher. I give him the voucher, we shake hands and I wish him well. I don't want to become numb to the problems I see, but there aren't ready answers to many of them.

## Scott

Scott is 27 years old, a high school dropout, arrested for auto theft at 18. He was released but arrested again for parole violation. He's been out for five months.

"Where are you staying?"

"At the men's shelter. I need an ID card to get a job." I see from his file that he's gotten IDs in the past and ask about it. "My wallet with my ID in it got stolen three different times at the men's shelter." He knows all too well the requirements to get a replacement card. He'll need to get sealed school and medical records to verify his identity. We complete the forms, and it's obvious he's tired. He's also hungry, having missed lunch this afternoon. I ask one of the permanent staff to get him some sandwiches, which she does. He tucks them carefully into his jacket.

He also has some medical issues. He had a kidney transplant, was prescribed medication, which he has in his bag, but hasn't been taking it regularly. "I don't remember all the time." I begin to feel that awful gnawing in my stomach I get when I meet someone like Scott. Chances are he's also suffering from depression and needs to see a doctor. I suggest he see the nurse tomorrow morning and request a referral to a doctor who can diagnose any mental health problems. "Thanks." He leaves. I hope he remembers to get his school and medical records.

## Jonathon

Jonathon was recently released from prison after serving a ten-month sentence for domestic violence. He's staying in a halfway house for convicted felons preparing to move back into the mainstream. He's been there for the last ten days. I ask how he likes the place, and he scowls in disgust, lifts up his shirtsleeve, and shows me his forearm. It's riddled with bedbug bites. "I have a hard time sleeping 'cause of dem bugs."

"Why don't you go the shelter?"

"I like this place better. Too many people hangin' 'round doing nothin' at the shelter."

He's here for assistance in getting his North Carolina ID. He's in good shape administratively to do this: he has his Social Security card, prison ID, and proof of residency from the halfway house. Most people who come in for IDs are missing some or all of this documentation. I give him a fee waiver and recommend he come back tomorrow to take the van to the DMV.

It's 100 degrees outside and Jonathon walked six miles to get here. He asks for a bus pass to get back and forth tomorrow, and I give him one. We talk for a while, and I ask, "What type of work did you do before prison?"

"Composer and music producer." He pulls out a flash drive from his pocket. "Want to hear some?" I eagerly nod, and we plug the drive into the computer. His music is very good. He's a very talented guy and I hope he can eventually take advantage of his gifts. I thank him for the chance to hear his music, and as we shake hands, I wish him well.

The arts are a notoriously difficult way to make a living. I wonder how many other talented artists have become trapped in the downward spiral of homelessness.

# Keith

Keith needs a replacement NC ID card. The police took his ID four years ago when he went to jail, and it expired. His jail ID would have worked as identification to get a state ID, but he threw it away when he was released. For the last three months, Keith has been living on the streets in parks, porches, and empty buildings. He's taken some steps to get his ID. He applied for a Social Security card three weeks ago but hasn't received it yet. It was to be mailed to a friend's home address. He'll also need proof of identity, such as sealed school records, and since he graduated from high school in Charlotte, getting them will be easier. I give him a school records request form to take to the school administration office. We call the Social Security office to learn the status of his card but can't get through to anyone. I give Keith the phone number I called and instructions on what to say so he can follow up. I ask him to come back here for a verification letter and waiver when he gets this stuff. As small as this seems, getting his ID will be a big win for him.

# Willie

Last night Willie slept in a dumpster. He was released from prison a few weeks ago on a felony charge and has lived on the streets since then. I ask why he doesn't go to the men's shelter. "I've had problems at the shelter, I can't stay there," is all he says. Surprisingly, he was able to find a job and just started work as a noncertified nurse assistant caring for eight clients. His records show a counselor called last week and verified the job with his boss. It sounds like he works at a facility for seniors and does some of the heavy lifting and dirty work.

"How do you deal with hygiene and tiredness from lack of sleep?"

"I've been showering here, and I've been getting enough sleep. I don't get paid till Friday, I need a bus pass to get back and forth to work this week." This is his second 10-way, and I tell him his last, since he'll start receiving a paycheck.

Willie's anxious to get into an apartment when he gets paid. He's making minimum wage and only working about 35 hours per week. It won't go far, but he may be able to get a subsidy or some assistance from another agency. I give him the pass and a list of agencies that may be able to offer some rent assistance and household goods when he gets settled. We shake hands, and I say, "Good luck, buddy."

# Larry

Larry just got a temporary job with a construction company and needs a 10-way bus pass to get back and forth to work until he gets paid.

"It's been hard to find work because of the economy and my record." I ask him about it, and he tells me he was released a few months ago after serving a felony sentence. "I was in for seven years and don't plan to go back."

"You're lucky to find a company that'll hire you." I ask for the phone number and verify the job with his boss. After hanging up, I ask Larry about his prison time. He doesn't want to talk about the charge or his time in prison, and I leave it alone. "You have an uphill struggle and can't afford any regression."

"I plan to stay clean and get on track. I want to earn enough to get my own place and out of the shelter." I hand him a bus pass and tell him he will be responsible for future passes. We shake hands and he leaves.

# Sam

He's short, about 5'5, with neatly cropped hair combed straight back accentuating his receding hairline. He has salt and pepper hair, hinting at his age and his eyes are a deep brown. There's a certain amount of sadness in his eyes that makes you want to ask, "what's wrong"? I don't want to start our conversation downstairs in the middle of the afternoon rush so I introduce myself and reach my hand out to shake. His name is Sam and he says he's been here before. "How's it going?" I ask as we begin our assent upstairs. He's looking down and shaking his head slowly back and forth and says" not so good, I'm havin some problems." I notice how soft spoken he is and wonder if he's a little depressed.

"Well lets get upstairs and see what we can do," I say, trying to be upbeat and confident. "Where you from?" I ask and he replies from Charlotte. We reach the office area and I ask for the last four digits of his social Security number. I type it in along with his name and up comes his profile. There aren't any notes from prior visits so I don't have anything to begin with other than to ask. I push my chair back and say, "what would you like to talk about today?"

"I been stayin in a hotel but I got to leave cause I'm out of money. I need to find a job and a place to stay and I'm havin a tough time with both. If I don't get a place to stay tonight the sheriff's gonna send me back to prison and I don't want to go there again." He unfolds his hands and moves his left arm toward his face to brush off a fly and I notice his hand and arm are mutilated. Half of his fingers are gone and the remaining stubs look as though they're fused together. His arm is darkly discolored up to his elbow and severely scarred. "What happened" I ask and nod my chin towards his arm.

"I got in an accident at work 15 years ago. My hand got caught in a piece of machinery I was workin on and I almost lost my entire arm. The doctor saved it for me and told me how lucky I was."

"Did you get anything from insurance?" I ask.

"Yeh I got a settlement but I went through that."

"Why is the sheriff so concerned about where you're staying?"

"I got outta prison in April and I have to let the sheriff know where I'm stayin."

"Why were you in prison? Is there a felony charge on your records", thinking this is the problem with his lack of success in landing a job.

"No it wasn't anythin bad. They put me in for not registerin."

"Are you an offender?" I ask, intentionally shortening the question for reasons I myself didn't understand at the time.

"Yes sir but it happened over 10 years ago."

The cloud lifts and now I understand what's going on. He's a sex offender and required to let the sheriff know where he's living and when he moves.

His record is public knowledge and a lot of employers aren't going to take a chance with a registered sex offender on their premises. " Are you aware there's an organization that helps ex convicts find work. They offer training on how to interview, complete resumes and network."

"No I don't know nothin bout an organization that does that. Where they at?"

"Lets look them up on the internet." I recalled the organization from a friend who volunteered there a few years ago. He asked me to speak to the group at a training session on how to interview and I gladly obliged. I couldn't recall the exact name of the organization but remembered they were located on the north side of town. I typed the words. Ex con training charlotte and up popped CCT, the Center for Community Transition. This was the organization I was referring to and we read their website together on the screen. "You need to call this number and make an appointment to enroll in their job training program. They give participants bus passes to get back and forth each day and train them on how to find a job and how to respond to tough questions."

"I'm gonna do that. I didn't know this place existed" he says excitedly.

"Well what type of work are you looking for?"

"I don't care. I do construction, cleaning,

warehouse work, anythin. I need to get a place to stay tonight cause I had to leave today. I been tryin to find some work but nobody is hirin. Everywhere I apply they don't have any openings".

"There's a lot of construction work in the city right now, mostly new homes. Have you tried to get on with a construction crew doing labor work? "

" I don't have no money to get there. There's no homes bein built in the city".

"I suggest you work through a temp agency that's hiring laborers for construction crews on a temporary basis. You can avoid having to go through a background check, which may impede your chances for a job at a lot of firms. You'll get paid weekly. The downside is you'll be paid less and won't have a permanent position. Upward mobility will be limited as will any tenure with a firm. I also recommend you call CCT and enroll in their program. It's a good one and you'll learn a lot from others in the program. Finally I think you should go to the shelter tonight and get a bed. I don't know if they have restrictions on offenders but you don't have other options at this point. Call the sheriff's office and let them know where you're staying also."

He sat and stared at the floor for a few seconds before lifting his head and thanking me for my time. "Are you here everyday?"

"No I'm here on Mondays and Thursdays. Why don't you stop in next Monday and let me know how you're doing?"

"I'd like to do that if it's OK" he says and lifts himself up from the chair. I stand and we shake hands and he leaves the office.

I sit down and try to put my thoughts together. There's a lot I don't know about him and never will. He's a human being that made a big mistake and now must pay for it. How much and to what degree? I could see the fear in him, his resignation to his future, and his lack of hope. Should he just go somewhere and die? I don't think so. It's going to be a hard day and another situation that doesn't have easy and readily available answers. He didn't come back the following week and I never saw him again.

## Louis

Louis's story is like an onion: the more you peel it back, the more it smells. He starts by telling me he isn't going to hold anything back and that he wants our meeting to be full disclosure so I can understand his situation.

"I'm here for two reasons. I need bus passes to get to my part-time job and one of those waivers you got to get my ID. I lost it last week." He explains he works two days a week earning minimum wage. I calculate he's earning about $5000 a year. "I've been living with my sister and want to get a place of my own."

"How long have you lived with your sister?" Eleven years. It doesn't sound as though he has investigated the costs of apartments. "You're making about $5000 a year. It's going to be tough to find a place you can afford with that income." He has an intensity about him that comes through his eyes. They widen when he talks and wants to make a point. I don't know if he's angry or surprised when he looks at me. He moves away from talk of the apartment back to his ID.

"I think you all have a copy of my ID here somewhere. See if you can find it."

I walk to the file room and look through his paper files for a photocopy of his ID. His file is thick and it takes me a while to find it. He was here within the last few months and the counselor he met with made a copy of his ID. When I return he asks, "What took so long? I almost left." He's starting to irritate me.

He calms down and begins talking about his job. He's looking for more work, but "Employers won't hire felons." First I've heard of any prison record. When I probe him about it, he says he was released from prison seven months ago after serving a 22-year sentence. "I haven't had a blemish on my record since being released. I've turned a corner in my life." He lied to me about how long he's lived with his sister, and I wonder what other lies he's telling. "I'm going to be a father for the first time in April. I need to get an apartment so my girlfriend and baby can live with me."

"How many children do you have?"

"This is my first. She gots seven other kids." I raise my eyebrows but he doesn't respond. I wonder if he is hoping to be able to care for all of them, but I don't ask. He doesn't want to go back to prison and reiterated that a number of times, and sitting here with him the short time we've been together makes me realize how difficult it will be for him to avoid it. He's 40 years old and has spent most of his life behind bars. He learned how to survive there, and prison culture has become a part of him. He's a prison-trained hustler trying to survive in a far different world. He needs more help than I can offer. He needs someone who can mentor him back into his new world and help him adjust. He has a Social Security printout, a copy of his ID, and the waiver I give him.

I recommend he come back Wednesday and speak with someone from the jobs program. There's a company that will hire without doing background checks, but the work is hard and laborious. In my opinion he doesn't seem to have that type of work ethic. He gets up and leaves without saying anything else. I go downstairs to get my next neighbor.

# Jay

He's spent almost a third of his life in prison and he's only 22 years old. Jay was released last month after serving six years. "I made a mistake, paid for it, and want to get on with my life." He seems fearful and in some respects delicate, and his polite and respectful demeanor distinguishes him. During our brief conversation, he talks about his mother, and I sense he has a deep love and respect for her. He wants to get a job and will need a North Carolina ID. He has a prison ID, and his school records and birth certificate are in Charlotte. It'll be difficult for a convicted felon to land a job but not impossible.

The jobs program has worked with a few firms that will hire recently released felons, and there are more than a few firms who will hire convicted felons if they've been clean for seven years or more. I give him the necessary forms to obtain his school records and birth certificate along with a folder to keep everything neat and clean. While helping him complete the forms, I ask for his father's name. He takes a deep breath while looking at the paper, pauses, and seems upset for a moment before giving me the name. He doesn't say more about his father, and I wonder silently what caused him to react in that manner but decide not to ask. I recommend he visit the jobs program next Wednesday and learn about some of the options available to him. He seems excited. He loosens up and tells me he lives with his girlfriend. He spends a few minutes talking about nothing in particular before we shake hands. He thanks me and I wish him well.

## Nick

He's a young kid with a friendly smile that hides his background. He's a recent parolee from prison, just eight days out and desperate to land a job and never go back. He got his NC ID yesterday and now wants a copy of his Social Security card. He doesn't need his card to get a job but wants it anyway. It's simple enough for him, and I explain what he has to do. I immediately take a liking to him. He has an easygoing demeanor and a sincere style that makes you enjoy helping him. I recommend he come to the jobs program. He's excited and writes a number of things he wants to do before Wednesday to prepare. I give him the necessary forms to waive fees and seek assistance, and shake his hand. He'll need some luck along with hard work.

# Felix

"How's it going," I ask as we walk upstairs to the office.

"Not so good. I need an ID."

We walk back to the office and sit down. He says he was here a while back, but when I look I can't find his record in the computer. "This won't take a minute," I say and begin asking the standard background questions to register him.

"I just got out of prison. I have a prison ID." He pulls it out and places on the desk. "And I can get my Social Security printout."

"Where are you staying?" At a halfway house not far from here but he doesn't remember the name. I've heard stories about prison halfway houses and ask, "Is it clean?"

"I think so, why?" I tell him about the neighbor who was bitten by bedbugs while sleeping in a halfway house. "No, this place is clean, no bugs that I seen."

"How long were you in?"

"Nine years." It's been a while since he was last here. I finish the personal input section of the registration and move on to emergency contacts. "I don't have no one."

"Mother, father, sibling, cousin, anyone?"

"My father killed my mother then killed himself. I been in prison so long no one ever wrote to me." I usually don't go forward with a registration until I get a name, but in this case I decide to move on.

I finish inputting the data and ask if he wants to talk about anything else beside his ID today. "I got a few medical problems. I got ulcers and been coughing up blood. Some mental problems too. Schizophrenia and anxiety."

The ulcers and coughing up blood sound serious. "How about going to the hospital right now?"

"I don't need to go now, it ain't bad enough yet."

I ask him to come in tomorrow and see the nurse. "She can refer you to a doctor for your ulcer and help you get medication and a specialist for your mental health problems." He says he'll think about it. He has another appointment tomorrow morning.

I wonder if he's being manipulative but I can't tell. I leave the office to get the waiver form and when I come back he's standing bent over coughing loudly. "You got anything for ulcers?" he asks.

"I'll check." I find a staff member with a key to the nurse's room and we both search for something to help him. The only thing available is a roll of Tums. I bring it to him and he takes three.

He sits back down. "Thanks, man, that'll help for a while."

I ask him to assure me he'll come back tomorrow. He finally nods and says he will. I ask again if he wants to go to the emergency room tonight, but he says the halfway house will help him get the treatment he needs. We stand and shake hands. I wish him well and he thanks me. I never see him again.

# Summary

Thirteen percent of the people I talked with openly admitted they were former prisoners, which presents one of the most difficult transitions from homelessness. For a majority of returning prisoners, their first home out of prison is with a family member, a close friend, or a significant other. Reunions like this aren't always possible or are only temporary because of family dynamics or court orders. For those who can't return to such a place, there are a few other options: transitional housing, special needs housing, the private market, and federally subsidized housing. The inventory of federally subsidized homes is very small, and when they are available, returning prisoners are usually at the bottom of the pecking order. In any case, few recent releases have the funds to pay for this type of housing. The same dynamics are true for special needs housing; law-abiding citizens have a far greater chance of being admitted when beds are available. Transitional housing is available for a limited time in some cases. Too many released prisoners find themselves in shelters or on the street, where the chances of returning to prison are the highest.

Added to this dilemma are the hiring restrictions many employers place on ex-convicts. A felon's wait time between release and hiring can be seven years or longer. Many prisoners work around this restriction through temp agencies, which generally don't check backgrounds or run security checks. The upside for the former prisoner is a chance to earn some money and possibly be hired permanently. The downside is the uncertainty these jobs have for the long term. It becomes a vicious cycle with little hope of breaking out. Some firms hire ex-convicts, but the positions generally offer minimum wage and little in the way of benefits.

Women have an especially difficult time. Often they must find a place for themselves and their children. The women's shelter in Charlotte requires a 90-day residency period before admission. The men's shelter in comparison has a greater inventory of available beds and only requires a 14-day residency.

Meanwhile, until they manage to get steady

employment, many ex-convicts stay in shelters. Studies have found that ex-prisoners who spend time in the shelter have higher rates of substance abuse, a greater chance of developing a serious health problem, and a more likelihood of reverting to crime.

# 5

# Substance Abuse

*Eric*

I FIND ERIC TO BE AN interesting person. When we first meet downstairs he seems aloof and nonchalant, but after I spend time getting to know him, he evolves into a very friendly and outgoing personality. He has a serious substance abuse problem involving both alcohol and drugs that's been with him most of his life. He wants to take a first start at kicking these habits by getting into the Rebound Program for substance abusers. The program is run by the Charlotte Rescue Mission and requires the individual call and enroll on his own behalf rather than a family member or friend doing so. Last Thursday he met with a UMC counselor who arranged a phone interview for Eric with a Rebound counselor. Eric was accepted into the program based upon the positive interview and was scheduled to show up there Monday to begin.

"I screwed up. Over the weekend I went out with some guys from the shelter, I don't want to call them friends, and got caught up in some stuff. I was afraid to go to the interview." He's also embarrassed and mad at himself as he discusses the situation with me. He went to Rebound anyway on Monday and told them what happened. The counselor advised him that if he went to the Charlotte detox center today, Rebound would admit him on Wednesday if he stays clean. "Will you call the detox center for me?" he asks sheepishly.

I call and learn they have beds available and will accept Eric immediately. They also verify what the Rebound counselor told Eric.

Eric doesn't have many options left in his life and to some extent he's at the end of the road. He estranged his siblings with his abuse problems and can't go home. His drug habit impacts him wherever he goes. He's lived in four states, one time studying to get a two-year degree in computer science, but due to a relapse, he quit the course and left the state. He had a skirmish with the law but wouldn't be specific. His story is the type that could end positively because despite his drug problems, he has a lot going for him.

When he leaves the office, he seems determined to succeed, but only time will tell. His journey will be difficult but not impossible, and I wish him the best as we shake hands.

# Nancy

Nancy's been coming to UMC for the last six years. She stays at a transitional home where she's required to take classes for a substance abuse problem. This is her ninth address in three years. She's also bipolar but taking medication to manage it.

She sits across from me while I pull up her info. Each neighbor's computer file has a page with a place for their photograph. Hers is a mug shot taken at the county jail last year. In it, her eyes are half closed and her hair is in complete disarray. It looks as if she just woke up and was surprised by the photographer. She sees it and gasps. "I didn't know they used that photo. Can you take that off?"

"I don't know how, but I'll try after our meeting. Anyway, it isn't printed or sent out. It's not out there for anyone to pull up."

"I don't care, I just don't like it." She settles a little, and I ask what she wants to talk about today. "I need some food from Loaves and Fishes but can't pick it up until Wednesday." Today is Monday. She has classes on Tuesday and the food center closest to her home isn't open until Wednesday.

"You going to be okay until then?"

"Just until then. I can't wait after that." I offer alternative meal locations but she declines. When she gets up to leave she gives me a hug and it makes my day. I try to remove the photograph but can't figure out how. I decide to leave it alone.

## Gregory

Gregory's a quiet and focused man who doesn't want to spend much time on small talk. He isn't abrupt but rather to the point. His answers to questions regarding his background are either yes or no. He has a court-ordered appointment and a court authorization letter to attend a drug-counseling program this week and needs transportation to get there. He's been coming to UMC on and off for the past two years. I give him two bus passes and he leaves quickly, without saying another word.

# Betty

When I meet Betty downstairs she's woozy and barely able to walk. The look in my eyes was enough for her to say, "I'm on medication for cirrhosis of the liver."

Startled, I say, "Let's ride the elevator upstairs."

"I can still walk," she says in a gruff voice and ambles upstairs to the office area.

I ask about the cause of her cirrhosis.

"I drank two fifths a day for a lot of years and it finally caught up with me."

For some unknown reason I ask, "Hard liquor or wine?"

"Both, but mostly wine because it's cheaper. I'm still addicted to alcohol, and I'm trying to beat it without joining AA."

She's 40 but looks 65. She asks for ice water and I get some from the kitchen. After taking a sip she asks for a Loaves and Fishes food voucher. She hands me a slip of paper that has June 4th written on it. She says when she came here May 3rd, she requested an L&F voucher for pickup on May 4th, but the counselor made a mistake and scheduled the pickup for

June 4th. The agency wouldn't give her any food as a result.

That story seems more than a little odd. I check her case records and see that she was here on May 3rd for an L&F food voucher. I've never heard of a counselor making that type of error before. I have her sit outside the office in a reception area while I call the L&F agency.

I explain the situation to the L&F volunteer and ask her to check their records. Betty had indeed made a food pickup on May 4th and signed for it. Betty's lying to me. She's either hungry and out of options or she's going to sell the food and buy some alcohol.

I call Betty back into the office and inform her about the record of her pickup on May 4th and that she isn't eligible for another until July 4th. She looks down at the floor, embarrassed, and acknowledges she made a pickup. I ask if she's hungry and needs to eat. Many places in the city provide meals during the day, including UMC.

"No, I have food, there isn't a problem." She's staying at a friend's house and they're both okay. She makes some small talk about her family situation, saying she has three children, two attending college and staying with their father and one child on her own. She stands to leave, and after wishing her well, I ask her to reconsider getting assistance for her alcohol problem. She casts her eyes down and says she'll think about it before she turns out the door. I never see her again.

# Carl

He sits in the chair across from me staring at nothing in particular. I ask what he wants to talk about today, and when he begins, he concentrates very carefully on his words and what he is saying. "I been using cocaine and alcohol for a long time..."

While he talks, his face contorts as if in pain. His body occasionally shivers, and he loses track of his thoughts. I can see the frustration on his face as he tries to recall the smallest of facts. He has particular memory problems with numbers and dates. He's going through withdrawal in front of me.

"Over the years my body adjusted, and I took more and more booze and dope to get the same level of high. Hell, I was drinking a fifth of liquor a day in the end and using cocaine all the time. If I couldn't find no liquor I'd drink two quarts of wine." He laughs. "One pint of liquor used to get me high, but my body got used to it and I began drinking a fifth to get the same feeling." He's been admitted to Hope Haven, a substance abuse center and halfway house that offers long-term housing for addicts. "I'll be in the program for two years." Hope Haven has a high success rate for addicts, and Carl is finally to a point where he's ready to take some proactive action to beat his addiction.

"My father was office manager for a carnival and I worked with a few carnival companies during my early years. It was hard but good work and I made decent money. I had a mobile home, and the wife and I would move from town to town with the carnival during the season." Eventually the nomadic way of life became too much, and they settled down in a small town in North Carolina. He owned a paint and body shop and was doing well enough to hire two or three employees. "I lost the business along with my wife and family when being high got more important than being safe."

Carl has a letter from Hope Haven acknowledging his entrance into the program, along with a requirement he get a copy of his criminal background report on his own before being fully admitted. He asks for a $25 check made out to the clerk of courts for the report. "My criminal report is so thick they might charge extra postage." After talking it over with staff, I give him the check. He reaches out for my hand and thanks me for listening and helping him. "Stop in when you come back and let me know how you're doing." I realize the odds are long, but I would love to see him pull this off. I never see him again.

# Jack

Jack sits down across from me and tells me he's in his mid-forties and been living at the men's shelter for the past three years. He was here last week, depressed and suicidal, and he couldn't shake the mood. "I thought I was losing my mind." He was lucky. He met an empathetic and understanding counselor who helped him get on a different track. He doesn't remember her name but he says she changed his life. I lean back in the chair as he continues.

"I've had an alcohol abuse problem for over twenty-five years. I was dishonorably discharged from the Navy in '86 because of it. I used to do landscaping, but for the last three years I haven't been able to find a regular job, just some occasional restaurant work washing dishes."

The counselor last week made him promise to go to the Billingsley mental health center to seek treatment, which he did, and he learned he wasn't as crazy as he thought. He met a psychiatrist who recommended he get off the streets, into a home, and find a job. I thought that was fairly obvious, but for some reason, it wasn't so obvious to Jack before that appointment. "That lady inspired me and I've been working hard to do that and turn my life around." I thought he may ask me for her name but he doesn't.

He's here today to find housing options, of which there are few unless you have an income. I recommend he look into alcohol abuse programs because some of them offer housing while going through a treatment process. Together we look at different programs online and one of them is at the men's shelter. It's called SACOT, Substance Abuse Comprehensive Outpatient Treatment. It's a 42-day program that offers structure and support to individuals as well as education and vocational skills that can lead to a job. It has a good success rate. I read it quickly and my mind races excitedly.

"If you're accepted into the program you'll have a guaranteed bed for the next forty-two days while you go through treatment. If you have stable housing you can look for a job as a landscaper or dishwasher, save some money, and begin to get back on your feet." I can feel his excitement about this possibility.

He confides that before moving to Charlotte he was seeing a therapist. "It was helping me deal with some of my issues," which he didn't get into. His family lives in Charlotte, and they asked him to come here. He had to quit seeing the therapist in order to comply. "Hindsight, I should have stayed."

I call the men's shelter to verify the program, and the administrator recommends Jack come over early and talk with him. Jack is intent on getting into the program and looks and sounds optimistic. I suggest he come back occasionally to see me and talk about his progress. We shake hands and I wish him well. I never see him again.

# Ed

Ed looks out of place in the waiting area. Light blue denim shirt, dark blue jeans, field boots, all neat and orderly, along with a slow southern drawl. He could be mistaken for someone working his farm.

This first impression is deceiving. He's homeless and has been for the last three years. He doesn't live on a farm; he lives in the streets. He's from Charlotte and has a daughter in town whom he lists as his emergency contact. He has a secret like everyone else. He has a substance abuse problem, and wants to get into the SACOT program at the men's shelter. First, he needs to get into the shelter. He has other secrets. He was married, but his wife threw him out years ago. I assume it was due to the substance abuse but I'm not positive.

"I have one additional problem I need your help with. I need to have a tooth pulled. It's been bothering me for a while. I'm taking some over-the-counter medication for pain and so far it's working but I don't know for how long."

"You have three options for the tooth extraction. The dental van will be here Friday, you can wait four days and try to see the dentist then. Your second option is to make an appointment to see a dentist at the men's shelter. Appointments are made on Thursday for the following Friday, which means an eight-day wait. Your third option is to go to the hospital and have it treated as an emergency."

He thinks about it quickly. "It's not an emergency yet and I don't want to use that option. Can you help me get an appointment for this Friday at the men's shelter?" I call on his behalf and learn they're completely booked. I make two suggestions. Get into the shelter today and make arrangements to get into the SACOT program. Then come Friday to the dental van, and if he can't get in, make an appointment the following Thursday at the men's shelter. He thinks that's a good plan and at that gets up, thanks me, shakes my hand and leaves.

## Tim

He's got a friendly smile and seems genuine as we shake hands downstairs and introduce ourselves.

"How's it going?" I ask as we walk upstairs to the office area.

"Pretty good, you know how it is, could be better, could be worse. The good Lord is watching over me and all I can do is have faith."

We reach the office and I check him in on our system before asking what he wants to talk about today. "I need a ten-ride pass to get back and forth to rehab."

"How long you been in rehab?" I go back to the computer and pull up notes from his last visit. I scan them quickly and see he was here last week for a ten-ride pass to rehab.

He smiles. "It'll be three months next week. I been stayin' clean, but I'll tell you, it's hard."

He's had a long-term drinking problem according to past notes and he's determined to break it. "Where are you staying?"

"At the shelter, been there for a long time. That's one reason I want to stay clean, so I can get a regular job and get a place of my own."

"Must be tough at the shelter. A lot of guys with time on their hands hanging around, it can lead to trouble if you aren't careful."

"I don't hang with the guys I used to anymore. I have a friend who doesn't live there. He's married and works. He gets paid on Friday, and we used to meet somewhere and go drink. He keeps askin' me to go with him and I don't. He works for a landscaper and said they may have a job opening. I'm afraid to because I'll start drinkin' again."

"It's never what you say to someone, it's how you say it. Why don't you be open with him and tell him you really like him a lot and want to be his friend. But you need his help. Explain how important this is to you and ask him to help you beat it. He can be part of the solution rather than part of the problem."

Tim had never quite thought of it in that manner. "Great advice, man." He reaches out to grab my hand and pumps it up and down. "I'm glad I came and saw you today. What's your name again?" I tell him. "You know what? My friend's married and his wife wants him to quit drinkin' too. She likes coffee. Maybe he and I can start drinkin' coffee."

"There you go." It's a feel-good moment for both of us. I get the pass for him and we shake hands again as he leaves to go see his friend.

## Sylvia

She's short, very short, with a warm cautious smile that puts me immediately at ease. I smile back and introduce myself. "I'm Steve. What's your name?"

"Sylvia."

"Let's go upstairs and get started." I turn toward the stairs. "How's it going?"

"Oh, fine, thanks to Jesus."

She's clutching a box to her chest that looks like it may have held a gift at some point. "What's in the box?"

She winks. "Wait till we get to where we're going and I'll show you."

In the office, I ask for the last four digits of her Social. Her name immediately pops up. She's been here once before, but there aren't any notes to accompany her visit. "What do you want to talk about?" I push away from the computer keyboard and smile. "More importantly, what's in the box?"

She grins, bends forward, and slowly pulls back the lid. Inside are plastic bracelets, beads strung on elastic bands. They come in many colors, some with letters on the beads that spell names or words. "I make these and sell them."

"Can I see them?" I ask.

She reaches into the box and begins to bring out pieces, placing them carefully and neatly on the table. She treats them as if they are made of gold, and I quickly surmise she knows a little about selling this stuff.

"I make these and sell them out of my car. Someone told me the police could stop me if I don't have a license to sell them." She pulls a piece of paper from her bag and places it in front of me. It's an application for vendor license from the city of Charlotte. I immediately think she wants some assistance to pay for it so I ask her if that's the reason for her visit today.

"No, I have the money to pay for it. I don't need no help with that. I want to know if I can use the Urban Ministry address on my license application."

"I don't see why not."

"Can you give me a sheet of letterhead paper that says I can?"

I tell her to wait while I get a blank piece of stationery and handwrite a note explaining this is her business address. I don't think this will be a problem, but I'm so enamored of this woman's drive and determination that I decide the risk if any will be slight. "How did you get into this business?"

"I've had a tough life, in and out of institutions and jail. I used drugs and was addicted at one point. I just decided to stop and make something of my life. I've been clean for five years but I'll tell you it's been hard. I'm glad I made that decision and stuck to it."

I ask what she means when she says institutions, thinking she may be dealing with mental illness.

"Treatment places to help me with the drugs. I was in jail a few times, but that's all behind me. I'm really excited about my bracelets." She explains what she's learned about purchasing the beads, what colors are selling well, and the importance of having enough vowels in the bead letters to fulfill her orders.

"You're becoming a real entrepreneur." She smiles broadly and nods. "How much are they?"

"Two dollars apiece."

"I'll take five." I reach into my pocket for some money and ask her to pick out five she likes, planning to give them to female volunteers and staff I work with.

She thanks me as she puts the letter in her bag. We shake hands and I wish her the best.

When she leaves I immediately walk over to a volunteer's office, explain the situation, and offer her a bracelet. She likes the bracelets and picks one for herself. I think Sylvia may be onto something.

## Summary

Of the people I talked with, eight percent openly discussed their substance abuse problem during our conversation. I'm sure there were other neighbors who were substance abusers and didn't discuss it with me.

With substance abuse, the question I ask myself is which comes first, substance abuse or homelessness? Some studies conclude the problems associated with substance abuse are too complex to completely determine which causes the other. Substance abuse can trigger homelessness in different ways. It can start with a gradual depletion of an individual's personal financial reserves, followed by job loss and a breakdown in family and friend relationships, and finally arrears on rent or mortgage payments, which leads to homelessness. Substance abusers often use their credit card to the limit before they are cut off. Borrowing money from family and friends to support a habit strains relationships to a breaking point.

Other studies conclude homelessness can lead to a life of substance abuse, especially among the young. There are a couple of reasons why people reach for drugs or alcohol when homeless. First, it's a way to cope with and escape their environment. It helps people temporarily forget about their immediate trouble but doesn't offer a long-term solution. Second, many homeless people become involved in the homeless subculture. They want to belong to something or somewhere and are looking for a sense of support and security. It's especially important to young people after losing their family relationships. Within the subculture there's a prevalence of drug and alcohol abuse, which is generally regarded as acceptable or even prestigious behavior. Another interesting finding is that people with a substance abuse problem tend to stay homeless longer than those without one.

Many of the people in the preceding stories want to kick the habit, and they start out on a quest to do so with the best of intentions. Unfortunately, it's difficult to beat it while living in a shelter or camp. Many of those who break out start in a disciplined supervised program away from other substance abusers. They're supported in different ways including mentorship, job training, job placement, and housing.

# 6

# Physical Injury/
# Medical Problems

## *Chris*

CHRIS LIMPS ACROSS THE ROOM WITH an outstretched hand to greet me. By the look on his face and his gait, he's in a lot of pain. I haven't seen him around before and suspect he's new. He asks if we can take the elevator to the second floor rather than walk the steps. While waiting for the elevator I ask how he's doing. He begins telling me his story.

"I had a bad fall at my job in a hotel last year, slipped on some grease that leaked out of something, and ended up getting spinal surgery. I've been on pain meds and going to physical therapy ever since." To compound his problem, his vision is also impaired, and he has difficulty bending and stooping. We reach the office, where he slowly and carefully sits down, relaxes, and exhales as though he's grateful for the seat and chance to rest. "I haven't had any money coming in since I fell and need some help to pay for my medicine." He shows me a prescription from the CMC pharmacy, which has a sliding scale program that allows a neighbor to receive prescribed medication at a reduced rate or for free, depending on income. We don't assist with prescriptions that contain a narcotic. I check online, and his prescription is fine. He also needs transportation to the Medical Center for physical therapy on Thursday.

"Do you have a lawyer?"

"I filed a lawsuit against the hotel, but mostly I want to get better and back to work." He had a position with a recycling firm that required significant travel. The combination of the work and travel was enjoyable for him and he has a strong desire to get back to his job. As we talk, he shares an interesting secret about his background. He's a Gullah from the South Carolina Coast.

I say, "I've spent a lot of time in the Charleston low country area and learned about the Gullah culture and heritage from locals." Gullahs are the descendants of slaves from the western and central parts of Africa. The language is English-based with African influence. Their descendants were brought through the ports of Charleston and Savannah. Almost half of all slaves brought to the United States came through Charleston. The cuisine along the Charleston coast is often called low country food and has a strong Gullah influence. It typically consists of vegetables, seafood, rice, and pork. Some other interesting Gullah descendants include Joe Frazier and Michelle Obama. "Can you speak the dialect?" I ask.

He says a few words in Gullah. Our conversation brings me back to the coastal area, and I recall the saltwater smell and the food associated with it. The conversation removes us temporarily from the harsh reality surrounding us. He's in good spirits and upbeat as he leaves. I give him bus passes and the sliding scale verification letter and wish him well as we board the elevator down.

# Andrew

This is Andrew's first visit to UMC. He's in a lot of pain from a fractured foot and walks with crutches. He has a prescription that needs to be filled for a pain-relieving drug that's classified as a narcotic. I tell him about our policy regarding narcotic prescriptions and that we can't help him get it. His best bet is the men's shelter, which has a medical area for neighbors to recover from injuries similar to Andrew's. He can get the necessary medication under closer supervision.

Andrew stays at the men's shelter but doesn't like it. "People harass me all the time. One time someone tried to steal my shoes and I caught them. Somebody else tried to steal my phone and sell it back to me."

"Why don't you leave?"

"Ain't got no other place to go."

All of this has a depressing effect on Andrew. I ask, "Are you feeling mildly bluesy or deeply depressed?"

"More bluesy than depressed but it still bothers me."

I recommend he see the nurse tomorrow morning. She can give him a referral to a specialist, and he'll be able to see a regular doctor who can follow up with his mental state and medical problems. I call the men's shelter on his behalf to inquire about admission into the medical area. I get an answering machine and leave a message for the director to call me. I explain the situation and leave Andrew's name. I recommend Andrew go to the shelter and ask for the director.

I also suggest that when he sees the nurse in the morning, he ask for a referral to the Samaritan House, a temporary home where injured homeless can stay for 10 days while they recover. It's not as long-term as the men's shelter, but the environment might be more appealing to him. Andrew needs to get off his feet for a while and heal.

## George

George is a 15-year naval veteran who served on an aircraft carrier in his last deployment before being honorably discharged. His demeanor and voice inflection make him an interesting conversationalist and someone whose company you can enjoy. He and his wife of 31 years recently came to Charlotte without a place to stay but with a lot of hope and aspiration; things haven't worked out as planned. They separated soon after arriving, and George is heartbroken, desperately wanting to get back with her. This is their second separation; the first one lasted 10 years. "It was a long time but we managed to sort through our problems and she came back." The primary problem this time is their homelessness. He stayed at the men's shelter the last four nights. I don't know where his wife stays but I suspect it's with friends.

His medical issues are numerous. He uses a cane to walk because of problems with his leg, hip, and arthritis. The limp is the result of a gunshot wound thirty years ago.

"A war wound?"

He shakes his head and looks away. The hip problem is the result of a malfunctioning replacement from a few years ago and needs to be replaced. His front teeth are missing on each side back to his incisors and he needs dentures.

Top priority for George is his marriage. "Do you offer marriage counseling?" I tell him we don't. "If I can get into a home or apartment and off the streets, I'm pretty sure my wife will come back." I nod and silently consider options. He'll need a North Carolina ID if he plans to stay here. He also needs help with an appointment at the VA hospital on Thursday. His wife took his car, and he doesn't think she'll drive him to the appointment, so he'll need bus passes.

We work together on a plan. I suggest he start with United Family Services. They offer marriage counseling at no charge and I hear it's good. Next I recommend he take advantage of free services the dental clinic offers by coming back on March 11th to ride the dental van to the clinic. I give him a DMV waiver to get his North Carolina ID tomorrow and recommend he come back to UMC on Wednesday when the VA representative is here. She could possibly help him with housing. Finally, I give him two bus passes for his doctor appointment on Thursday.

George is a decent person going through some major issues at a time when he should be enjoying life more. He's 60 years old and not yet eligible for Social Security. He plans to wait until he's 66 to receive the full amount, but I don't think that will be a wise choice for him and suggest he look at the income impact at different ages. He's been here for a while and wants to get back to the shelter to ensure he has a bed tonight. We walk together downstairs. He thanks me; I wish him well and silently hope things work out for him.

## Karen

Karen is an interesting person. Born and raised in Harlem, she moved to Virginia after high school and lived there for a while before coming to Charlotte. She has severe asthma and is unable to work. She's trying to get a monthly disability check from Social Security, which would amount to approximately $800. She stayed at the Salvation Army women's shelter when she first arrived in Charlotte. "The shelter has a curfew rule and everyone who stays there needs to be in the shelter by ten. I missed curfew twice and ain't allowed to come back for sixty days."

"Where are you staying?"

"Outside, wherever I can find a safe place to lie down."

"How long have you been doing that?"

"Since April." Three weeks. She's not a drug or alcohol abuser and therefore doesn't qualify for transitional housing for addicts. Before moving to Charlotte, she suffered physical and mental abuse by her boyfriend but doesn't qualify for transitional housing for battered and abused women because her boyfriend's in jail. We call two women's shelters located in towns just outside of Charlotte, but both are very small and only take residents from their respective towns. There are very few affordable housing options for the homeless. I give her the name of the manager of Moore's Place. I would normally make this call, but Karen will be better able to explain her circumstances and be more compelling. It would be a long-term solution but it's a long shot. If nothing else, she can complete the vulnerability index, which will determine her eligibility for admission in the future.

Our last option is to call the Salvation Army women's shelter and ask for a reprieve. I make the call, but the director isn't there and the operator suggests Karen come in the following morning to meet with the facility administrator. Karen isn't hopeful about this option; she tried it twice before but to no avail. She's not allowed back into the women's shelter until late June, which is 40 days away. I sit there and consider what I would do in this situation.

"I'm afraid there aren't many options for you until then." She realizes the hopelessness of her situation and leaves the office. I sit there and shake my head out of frustration.

# Mickey

Mickey is handicapped and gets around on a scooter. He lives at the shelter and is anxious to get into a place of his own. We ride the elevator to the office and sit across from each other. For the first time, I look at him closely. I start talking with him but can't help but notice he has an awkward stare and facial expression that make me think he doesn't comprehend what I'm saying. He seems to churn every word I say in his mind until the sounds come together and make sense.

"What do you want to talk about?"

"I found four apartments I can afford on my disability income and want to have a look at them." He gestures down at his legs and scooter. "To see if there's any physical problems."

"Are you aware the transit authority has a special van for the handicapped?"

He seems startled. "For real?" I look it up online and download an application for the service. The length of the application at eleven pages surprises me. Mickey's grateful, doesn't care about the length, and says he'll fill it out and mail it in tomorrow. I begin to wonder if the facial expression had to do with something else less obvious. He seems perfectly fine now. "I still want to go see the apartments now rather than wait for the application to be approved. Can you give me bus passes?"

I feel awkward since he's handicapped. "We normally don't do that, but I'll make an exception this one time. You'll need to make other arrangements in the future." He thanks me, and we shake when he gets onto the elevator. I wave to him as the door closes. I feel sorry for this guy and consider making a bigger donation to UMC in the future to make up for the extra passes.

## Jarrett

He sits across from me, and from first glance, I like him. He has a friendly face and a warm smile. He hands me an acceptance letter from Hope Haven, an organization that provides a residential environment for people with disabilities and substance abuse problems. The letter says that besides a room, he'll receive vocational and workforce training, which is a primary motivator for him. He needs $25 for a background check as a condition of acceptance, and asks if we can give him the money. He also requests a bus pass to get to and from the county jail for his background documents.

"It's only a few blocks," I say, "why don't you walk?"

"I have a sore back and can't walk far."

I leave the office to see a staff person who will need to approve the expenditure and is also more familiar with Hope Haven. He approves the expenditure, and his eyes open wide when he sees Jarrett's name.

"I know Jarrett, he's a great guy and I'm glad to see he's making some good progress." The staff member has been working with Jarrett for a while. "Jarrett and his wife are trying to figure things out so they can live together. She works in the suburbs and commutes back and forth on public transport to the women's shelter. Jarrett's been at the men's. They can't afford their own place on her income alone. He's been sick on and off and has some unusual physical problems so he can't keep a steady job. And a heart condition that ate up a lot of their income." This helps me better understand Jarrett's situation. The check is cut and I give him the bus passes. I wish him well, and he leaves upbeat.

# Carmine

Last week my counseling sessions were grim and discouraging, and I come today hoping for better. My first session this morning is with Carmine. He looks happy when I meet him downstairs. I ask how it's going. "Just great," he says, which is unusual on a Monday.

On the walk upstairs I learn he's from Charlotte. I ask for the last four digits of his Social, and his name pops up on the screen along with his picture. In the office he's wearing a stocking cap with salt and pepper hair sticking out from both sides. He looks fit in his cloth bomber jacket, wearing a big smile and wire-rim glasses. He's missing one of his teeth, but somehow that just adds character to his appearance.

After examining notes from his last visit, I turn and ask, "What do you want to talk about today?"

"I just moved into a new apartment I've been waiting on for the last two years."

"Congratulations!"

"Yeah, they tore down the old apartments and built these new ones, and I got an efficiency." *They*, I learn, is the Federal Housing Authority, and the complex he's talking about consists of affordable housing units not far from here. Carmine had been living in the shelter off and on for the last two years and is glad to be out. He just turned 65 last month.

"Now I need a mattress and some furniture. I been sleeping on the floor and I hurt all over."

"Do you have any income?"

"I get a disability check each month, nine hundred."

"How much is your rent?"

"It's subsidized. I pay two forty-five."

Number one, two, and three on his list of needs are a bed, box spring and mattress. I leave to get the necessary forms for Crisis Assistance and we fill them out together. I explain the process, and stress he'll be responsible for arranging pickup of the furniture.

"I don't know no one with a truck," he says.

"They don't deliver and the only other option is to hire someone to pick it up. From the time you're approved and pick out what you want, you have three months to arrange for a truck to pick it up."

"I'll find someone. Can I get a sofa, chair and dinette set too?"

"It depends on what they have but I don't see any reason why you wouldn't be approved. If they don't have anything now, you can go back later and look." I fax the form to Crisis and instruct him to call after three days to arrange an appointment.

"Thank you so much." He stands, shakes my hand, and leaves the office. I'm feeling good about today.

# Summary

Seven percent of those I talked with had physical or medical problems that prevented them from working. Some had been hurt on the job, others in accidents, and some were just worn out. Degenerative diseases accompany old age, which can lead to homelessness. These people lack a financial safety net to insulate them from this type of catastrophe and consequently end up in the shelter or on the streets.

They want a place of their own, nothing fancy, but away from the shelter, someplace they can live without fear. They need access to prescriptions and medical care. The only income some have is a small disability check from Social Security. Some are veterans, who are always referred to the veteran's hospital.

Often medical problems precede and contribute to homelessness, and occasionally they are the consequence of homelessness. In most cases, homelessness complicates the treatment of injuries and illnesses and frequently worsens them. I often hear stories about fights and scuffles, and meet people with lacerations, cuts and bruises. Homelessness increases the risk of certain types of medical problems and injuries such as dental disease, joint disease, cirrhosis, and physical assault and trauma.

Job-related accidents are common among the people in this group. Programs such as Workers

Compensation, which was designed to prevent economic devastation, often fall short. In some cases the level of benefits are too low, and in other cases there just aren't any benefits for those who work off the books. Without an economic safety net or family and friends to lend support, the injured or ill often become homeless.

Providing medical care to the homeless is especially complicated. Take the case of a diabetic: if they require insulin, they may lack refrigeration to store it, and when injecting themselves, are often mistaken for addicts. Even bed rest is troublesome—shelter residents must leave early in the morning, and when I see them they are usually tired and lethargic. Some shelters provide an area for neighbors who are recovering from an injury, but there are never enough beds or resources. If they require a special diet they can't get it. Soup-kitchen food is mostly filling, not necessarily wholesome. Prescription drugs are available but are often stolen.

# 7

## Divorce/Poor Home Life

*Patrick*

PATRICK IS A 19-YEAR-OLD HIGH SCHOOL student. He left a very volatile home environment, filled with substance abuse and other serious problems, and is living with a friend on a temporary basis. He tells me he likes computers and has dreams of someday going to college and getting a degree in information technology.

He brings a copy of his current high school transcripts. Unfortunately, they're not good. Although you can see improvement year to year, the majority of his letter grades are failing. He blames this on his homelessness for the past four years and talks about the difficulty he had studying.

Despite his home life, he has some good things going for him. He doesn't use drugs or alcohol or have a police record. He's a member of the high school track team, running the 200-meter and throwing the shot put. He has a male mentor at school who is trying to help him as an advisor and a positive role model. Although he doesn't volunteer the identity of the mentor, I suspect it's a teacher.

He needs a state identification card. He has a current school photo ID, and with his transcripts as well, he'll be able to get a copy of his Social Security card. He was born in Charlotte, which will make it easier for him to get a copy of his birth certificate. I give him the necessary forms and paperwork to get his Social Security card. We'll send for his birth certificate and have it delivered to UMC, where he can check in the mailroom beginning next week. I advise him to come back for a DMV waiver letter after he gets his Social Security card and birth certificate.

I try to be encouraging, but it's hard to do in a short time, not to mention I'm old and white and he's young and black. I really like this kid but he has a tough road ahead of him. Not impossible, but tough.

# Arthur

This is Arthur's first time being homeless, and it's gone on for a month. As I register him into the system, I ask for an emergency contact.

"I don't have no one to give you."

I hate to accept that as an answer and silently think *we're going to sit here until you do.* It's a depressing circumstance to think no one cares whether you live or die, and I want to force him to think about it a little harder. In the end I usually get a name. "Is your mother or father alive?"

"No."

"Any siblings?"

"Two brothers, but we don't talk." He finally gives me the name of his uncle, who stays at the same shelter Arthur does. Arthur has an interesting story. "I left home because my wife ran off with one of my brothers. She told me she was pregnant and my brother was the father." While he struggles to tell me the story, I struggle not to look shocked. "I had to get away from there, so I came here."

"How did you end up at the shelter?"

"My uncle was staying there and he helped me." This story is missing a lot of parts, and I would love to delve into them, but I suspect from his body language he doesn't want to rehash all of it with me.

"What do you want to talk about today?"

"Someone stole my wallet at the shelter and I need a new ID to get a job." Fortunately, he has his birth certificate and Social Security card. I give him a DMV waiver and ask if he wants to talk about anything else. He hesitates for a couple of moments then says, "No," reaches out for my hand and shakes it. When he leaves, I sit down and stare outside for a while trying to digest his story.

# Donna

Donna's been homeless for the past two years, staying with friends or living on the street. She recently received custody of her 17-year-old daughter from her ex-husband who lives in Washington D.C. Her daughter's a victim of physical and mental abuse by her father. Both Donna and her daughter have mental health issues that require medication. Donna says her daughter is a "cutter" and describes the scars on her arms and wrists from various self-inflicted cuts and attempted suicides.

Donna is also HIV positive and a former substance abuser. She's been clean for a number of years but has a long history of drug and alcohol abuse.

"I need to get into a shelter and off the streets with my daughter," she says in a polite but concerned tone. She also wants to ensure her daughter finishes high school, receives her diploma, and hopefully gets into college. Even with the abuse her daughter has suffered, she has been able to maintain a 4.05 grade point average on a five-point scale for three years.

"That's remarkable," I say. Donna, obviously proud of her, beams.

I ask her to enroll in the sliding scale program through the hospital pharmacy to ensure she and her daughter receive their medication. Since they have no income now, the medication will be given at no charge.

I give her the address and phone number of the women's shelter, and we call while we're together. She learns she's eligible for emergency shelter, and hopefully they'll be able to stay there until she gets settled with a job or permanent housing. We then look online for tuition assistance programs for local schools and colleges. I show her online sites and how to investigate the possibilities. She'll be able to follow up on her own at the library.

In spite of everything she has been dealing with, Donna seems to possess a positive, can-do attitude. She has a lot of work to do.

## *Laura*

She seems out of place, a white middle-aged woman's face in a sea of men. She stands, and her clothes and makeup say volumes about her. She's neatly dressed, hair nicely fixed up, and even has some polish on her nails. At first I think she's a volunteer but learn she's a neighbor.

"I'm Steve." I reach out to shake her hand.

"Laura. Thanks for seeing me."

She leads the way up the steps. She's from Pittsburgh and just moved here. "What brought you to Charlotte?" I ask.

"There wasn't any work for me up there and I *had* a friend here who offered to help me." The "had" seems intentional but I let it pass for now.

"Have you been here before?" She says no. I start to register her into the system. "Who do you want to have called in case of an emergency?"

She hesitates. "Do I really have to give you someone?" I nod and wait. "I have two sons who live in the Southwest, but they don't know I'm here today and I don't want them to find out."

"They won't, not unless there's an absolute emergency." She gives me the name and number of the elder. I finish the registration, pull back from the computer and ask what she wants to talk about.

"I need a place to live. What are my options?"

"Do you have a job?" Part-time, 20 hours a week at a grocery store. "How much do you make?" $8.25 an hour—roughly $8,500 per year, not enough to get an apartment and eat.

"I just got a second part-time job at McDonalds at the same pay. I begin next week. Between the two, I think I can afford an apartment."

"Where are you staying now?"

"At a friend's house but I have to leave by the end of the month." At the word friend she raises her eyebrows as though the word was forced into her mouth and tasted like mud. "I've been there for three months and they told me they feel they are enabling me. They've asked me to leave."

She begins to open up and tell me more about her past. She had a life of mental and physical abuse by her former husband in Ohio. They lived very comfortably in a large home and had a big income. All that was lost with their divorce. Her former husband remarried, started a new family, and has nothing to do with his two sons from their marriage. "He hasn't talked with them in years. They were heartbroken initially but now they've grown to dislike him."

I look online for rooms to rent and find a few options. She looks at one grouping in particular and excitedly says, "Any of those would work just fine." I suspect she's more concerned about not ending up at the shelter than other considerations such as safety or convenience. I move to another section of subsidized homes and apartments for the poor. She will be eligible for a rent subsidy at her income level. "Could you print out those pages for me?"

I do so and hand them to her. "You know you'll eventually have to tell your kids what's going on."

"I will when I get settled." She still feels she needs to be strong and isn't ready to ask her sons for help. We shake hands, and she thanks me as she leaves the office. I sit back down and say a prayer for her.

## Kim

I'll never forget Kim. When I meet her downstairs, we exchange introductions, shake hands, and begin the walk upstairs to the office area.

As usual, I ask, "How's it going?" as we step along.

"I just got out of prison yesterday and need an ID."

"Let's get to the office, enter your information into the system, and start working on getting that ID." She has a warm smile and seems genuine in every way. I begin the entry process, and when we reach the prior housing section, I ask, "How long were you in prison?"

"Fourteen years." She's very matter-of-fact, no apologies, no excuses.

"What were you in for?"

"Murder."

Fourteen years doesn't add up to a murder charge. "Don't you mean manslaughter or some other type of charge?"

"No, I murdered him. It was premeditated. I'm writing a book about my life, what happened, and why I did it."

I stop typing and push my chair back. "Where's the book?"

She reaches into her bag, pulls out a pile of papers, and hands them to me. "Right here. I want you to put it into my file."

"Do you mind talking about what happened?'

"I was orphaned in Kenya when I was ten years old. My mother and father were killed and I was sent to an orphanage in London. I was adopted by a family in the United States. They lived in Kansas."

"Sounds fortunate."

She gives me a tight smile. "The man sexually abused me. His wife wouldn't listen to me and didn't believe me."

"So you killed him?"

"No, I ran away. Hitchhiked on the Interstate and a truck driver picked me up."

Expecting the worst, I ask where he brought her.

"To Charlotte. He dropped me off at the bus station."

I try to phrase my concern delicately. "Were there any...problems with him during the trip?"

"He was nice to me and even gave me some money when I got here. I told him what happened and he treated me good all the way here."

"So what did you do when you got to Charlotte? Did you know anyone here?"

"I met a woman who became my friend and let me stay at her house. She helped me get a job in a restaurant and then at a club. Then she introduced me to this guy she knew, and I started using drugs and got hooked on coke. I started selling myself to buy drugs."

I sit transfixed. She looks at me as if maybe I've heard enough. "Go on," I say.

"I got pregnant, and after I had the baby, I quit working at clubs and got a job at a restaurant. I wanted to change my life. I also got my GED. I didn't want my daughter to go through the same thing I did."

"It must have been very difficult."

"I always had at least two jobs to make ends meet. I'd have different men friends who stayed with me and sometimes helped me with money. Can I have a glass of water?"

I scurry off to get it. She picks up when I return.

"My daughter stayed in school until tenth grade, when she got pregnant. She told me it was one of the men who stayed at my house. He raped her one day while I was at work and she never said nothing 'bout it to me."

"Did you tell the police?"

"No. I wanted to get even myself."

"What did you do?"

"It took me almost a year. He never knew she told me 'bout the rape and all. I'd see him around and he'd talk with me, but he never knew my daughter told me what he did. I finally went out with him, and we were at his place, drinkin' and takin' some stuff. I was givin' him oral sex and he let me tie him to the bed. He didn't know I had a razor blade with me. He was high and tied up. I took the razor blade out of my pocket and cut his dick almost clean off. "

I moved back in my chair. "What happened then?"

"He was screaming but no one could hear him. He bled to death on the bed. Then I called the police."

I nod my head in an understanding way, unsure what to say. "Thank you for telling me your story…it should make a compelling book."

"They arrested me and I ended up in prison. I'm still glad I did it."

169

I return to the computer screen and give her the waiver and instructions on what to do at the DMV. "I'll put your book in your file, and if you need it, you'll know where it is."

She gives me her big warm smile again. "Thank you."

When she leaves, I file her manuscript in her folder. I never see her again.

## Summary

Divorce can be exceptionally cruel for a spouse who stayed at home with the kids, especially in middle- and working-class families. They lack up-to-date job skills and have a difficult time earning enough money to support themselves and, often, the children. Financial support from the noncustodial spouse can evaporate for a number of reasons: they can move out of state or out of country, lose their job, or die. This is especially hard for older people.

A poor home life can have similar consequences. Arthur lacked support from his family and he didn't have any savings. Patrick started off on the wrong foot by lacking a good role model at home; fortunately, he may have found one at school. Donna lacked support from family and friends and didn't have any savings. Laura is a classic example of what happens when financial support ends from a former spouse. All good people caught in a catastrophic event that eventually led them to the Urban Ministry for help.

# 8

# Other/Don't Know

## Daniel

DANIEL RELOCATED TO CHARLOTTE FROM THE southwest and has a horrific story to tell. Two months ago, his wife, in her sixth month of pregnancy, died in an automobile accident at the hands of a drunk driver. He was devastated and left his home to move to Charlotte. The drunk driver with a history of DUI arrests was convicted of first-degree murder and received a life sentence. I begin to feel sorry for him and nod in affirmation for him to continue.

He leans back in his chair and puffs up his chest. "I have friends in prison who'll eventually take care of him." I'm taken aback by this statement. Why does he have friends in prison? What type of friends does he have? What did they do that landed them in prison? Does "take care of him" mean what it sounds like?

Daniel tells me he tried to kill the driver while visiting him in jail. My suspicions deepen and more questions arise as he continues talking. How did he gain access to the driver? How did he try to kill him? I ask Daniel if he intends to sue the drunk driver. His answer surprises me even more than the previous statements.

"I don't want no part of him, or of any of my life before she died. I gave her sister our house, a hundred acres of land, and my new Dodge truck. Done. Gone." He signs deeply. "Then I came to Charlotte." I have no idea how much if any of this I can believe.

He came to UMC today for two reasons. The first is to obtain some form of proof of citizenship. North Carolina requires a Social Security card and proof of citizenship in order to get an ID card. He has his Social Security card and an expired driver's license. The North Carolina DMV wouldn't accept the expired license and advised him to get a valid proof of citizenship, such as a birth certificate, passport, or a marriage license. Daniel was born in another state, and in my experience, an out-of-state birth certificate can take as long as six weeks to arrive. Daniel never had a passport, and getting one will take longer than a birth certificate. I recommend he use his marriage license and ask if he still has it. He says it's at his old house. I suggest he call his sister-in-law and ask her to send it to him.

"She won't do that for me."

"Why not, especially after your generous gifts to her."

He silently looks out the window. I suggest he try to contact his sister-in-law anyway and ask her before we start the process of sending for his birth certificate. He says he will.

He asks for bus passes to get to his job. He says he works for a company through a temp agency and gets paid every Friday. He'll begin purchasing his own bus passes once he gets paid. I explain we first have to verify the job and ask for the name of the temp agency.

"I work for three temp agencies."

"I need the name of the one that's going to pay you Friday."

"It's in my backpack downstairs. I'll go look." Just as quickly, he changes his mind and says he has another way to get to the job site. He leaves my office rather abruptly, and I decide to check him out on-line.

The Internet is a wonderful tool for this type of work. After a few inquiries, his name pops up in a search through his home state. He's a registered sex offender and a convicted felon for armed robbery. I suspect he didn't register as a sex offender in North Carolina and I plan to report him. He and his mother were arrested in 2009 for armed robbery, and he served time in prison for two separate offenses. I doubt his entire story and wonder if he was ever married. He is one of the very few people I meet as a counselor who is just not a good person.

## Mark

As I walk downstairs prepared to leave for the day, I spot a young man nervously looking up at me from the bottom of the steps. Without his saying anything, I know he's waiting for a counselor. The front desk volunteers sign up four neighbors for each counselor, which is the average number of people one counselor can usually work with in a day. I ask the front desk about him, and it turns out this young man didn't make the original cut but needs some assistance. The volunteer introduces me to Mark and explains he has a doctor appointment tomorrow morning at 10:00 in the university area, which is some 10 miles from the shelter where he's staying. She already verified the appointment with the doctor's office. He needs bus passes for the roundtrip to the doctor's office.

I haven't done the usual interview, but the office is closing. I run back upstairs and get two bus passes for him. He genuinely thanks me and leaves for the shelter.

# Kevin

Kevin lives at the men's shelter. He recently landed a job at the airport refueling planes. He underwent a rigorous background check and training regimen and is ready to begin refueling planes on his own this week. He is concerned about living at the men's shelter. He will work the late shift, getting back to the shelter around 2:00 A.M., and worries a bed won't be available at that hour. The shelter hasn't confirmed he will have a regular bed, which means he may have to sleep on the floor or wait until someone gets up and take his bed. He wants to find a place near the airport he can afford and be able to walk to work. He makes $8.50 an hour and figures he can buy a bike and ride it to the airport from a nearby place. Originally from the Northeast, he worked for a time as a baggage handler at another

177

airport. He is 53 years old. I show him how to go online, which he can do at the library, to search for inexpensive rentals.

He asks for a 10-way bus pass meanwhile in order to get back and forth to work until payday. Each way is a 45-minute bus ride. I give him the 10-way and wish him well.

## Frank

He starts by telling me he recently accepted a full-time job in a warehouse and needs a bus pass to get to work tomorrow. He's nervous and won't look me in the eye, which makes me suspicious.

"When are you getting paid?"

"Not exactly sure…"

I ask the name of his boss and a phone number so I can verify his employment."

"I forget, I just know how to get there by bus."

"Why aren't you asking for enough bus passes to get to work until payday?"

His eyes light up. "Hey, that's a good idea, let's do that."

I move to the computer and begin looking for the address and phone number of the company he said gave him a job.

"What are you doing?"

"Calling to verify your employment. We have to do that before giving out bus passes."

He gets up and leaves the room.

Frank is a poor liar, which won't help him on the street either.

# Margaret

I ask neighbors where they're from when I first meet them to break the ice and find some common ground. Margaret tells me her father's a retired military officer who served in Europe for a time, and that her birthplace is Naples, Italy. She and her family moved to the United States when she was seven. I explain my family originated not far from Naples in a little town called Baiano.

"Oh, sure, I know Baiano. It's beautiful. We used to go to Italy a couple of times a year to see friends." She tells me she's currently working on a construction project at the airport as a laborer, tearing down an old parking deck and building a new one.

As she talks, I check her record. She's been coming to the Urban Ministry since 2003, primarily for prescription medication and food. This time she's in need of food. I schedule a food pickup, and when she leaves, she waves cheerily. "Ciao!"

Her file is on the desk and as I pick it up to refile

it I decide to review it. Her birth certificate is in it. To my surprise, her birthplace is New York, and her father is a retired salesman for a major technology company. I sit and stare at her file for a few moments. Her story, however fake, meant something to her. She may have some deep emotional problems that need to be addressed.

# Peter

Peter has a job as an assistant chef at a local restaurant, working there since February. He's making approximately $35,000 per year and has a few thousand dollars in a bank account. He's still living at the men's shelter. I ask him why.

"I'm saving my money to bring my fiancée to Charlotte. She's pregnant and I want to make sure we'll have a place to live when we marry and the baby comes." He also asks me for bus passes to get to his doctor appointment tomorrow.

I sit and stare at him for a long moment. What is he thinking? "You don't belong at the men's shelter, and for sure you don't meet any of the qualifications to get free bus passes from UMC. Go to your bank and withdraw money to buy them." I struggle to maintain a measured tone of voice.

He smiles apologetically. "I knew it was a stretch, but what the hey."

"Quit taking advantage of the system and get on with your life and new family." He jumps up and leaves immediately.

I tell a few staffers about this and none of them have ever heard of someone living in the men's shelter to save money. Too many genuinely homeless people actually need our help.

# Doug

Doug is 19 years old and a high school dropout. He was referred here by the Social Security administrative office for help in obtaining his state ID. His mother, whom he left sitting downstairs, is driving him from appointment to appointment.

"Do you know," I say, "that we deal primarily with homeless people?"

His expression quickly moves to shock, then extreme discomfort. He seems about to bolt. I try to calm him by assuring him we can assist. Doug needs a copy of his Social Security card or proof of his Social Security number in order to get his driver's license. He lost the original but remembers the last four digits.

"I'm worried someone will find my card and use it to create a phony ID."

"Check your credit rating occasionally. My sense of it is that you would already have heard something from creditors if that happened." I give him the necessary letter and directions to obtain a sealed copy of his school records, which he'll need to get a copy of his Social Security card. Mom will be driving him from place to place today because he plans to get his driver's license tomorrow.

"Good luck, buddy," I say as he sheepishly leaves the office.

## Terry

Terry lost his wallet yesterday with all of his identification. He's a Marine vet from New York. He's going to need two different types of supporting documentation in order to get a new ID. He graduated from high school in New York, so we call the school to get his school records, but it's closed for the day. He says he'll call the school tomorrow and ask them to send him a sealed copy. Tax records are another document he can use, and he says he'll find those at home.

"Come back when you get your documents together and get a fee waiver from us." He nods agreeably and we begin to talk about the Corps. He and I were both in the Marine Corps in the 70s and we have some common memories. I don't see a lot of vets at UMC, and I'm glad. In the end we shake hands and I wish him the best. He thanks me and leaves.

# Gerald

Gerald's library card expired and the librarian told him to come here for a homeless verification letter in order to get a new card. This seems odd to me, so I check the instructions for library card renewal online. An individual needs a current valid state ID in order to get a library card, and Gerald has one, but his ID shows the Urban Ministry address. The librarian must know this and doesn't feel comfortable with it for some reason. He uses the UMC address because this is where he gets his mail. I call the administrative office of the library to ask why his current ID isn't appropriate, but they're all off today. I speak with an operator, but she's unaware of the process or procedure.

I give Gerald a homeless verification letter he can bring to the library. I say, "It doesn't make sense to me either." I suspect the librarian is following procedures as she understands them, but I feel for Gerald and the hassle he and other homeless neighbors are regularly put through.

# Ralph

Ralph just turned 21 and wants a NC ID. He isn't very talkative and only lets me know he lives with his mother. He's not sure how to get his ID and wants direction. He has his Social Security card, and since he was born in Charlotte, he'll be able to walk to the downtown records office and get a copy of his birth certificate. He doesn't ask for help to pay for the certificate. I explain the process, give him a waiver, and hand him a map of how to get to the nearest DMV office. The entire meeting takes ten minutes. He quietly says thanks as he leaves with the form and map.

# Jim

Jim moved here from the Midwest to seek a better life, and it isn't working out as planned. Today, at 61, he's homeless and in his twelfth month of living in a camp on the outskirts of the city. Seven years ago he had a steady job as a certified nurse, solidly entrenched in the middle class with a home, automobile, family, and a decent income.

He doesn't say a lot about his past. "Things have a way of changing on you." Surprisingly, he seems upbeat with a cheerful smile that stretches across his face from ear to ear. He's been here before, and I review his history.

He came today out of a number of needs; the most urgent is to get a letter from UMC that affirms he's homeless so that he can continue receiving free medication from the hospital pharmacy. Other needs include an eye exam, eyeglasses, assistance to obtain dentures, and food. Food is a close second priority for James, and he requests a Loaves and Fishes voucher. In a camp environment, perishable food is hard to maintain, and most recipients living in a camp request canned goods. If the camp is near a cool stream and a cooler is available, some food can be stored for a short time. James doesn't discuss the type of food he'll request.

I give him the verification letter and schedule his food pickup. I fax a request for an eye exam to the Lions Club, which can take up to four months to schedule because of lack of resources and increased demand. The dental van and pro bono dentists come here the second Friday of each month, and they should be able to help him with the dentures.

## Mary

Mary had been staying at the Salvation Army women's shelter until she was asked to leave in November.

She has slept at various churches each night since then through the Room at the Inn program. This is Mary's first time at UMC, and I sense there's a lot to know about her and her stay at the women's shelter. She doesn't care to discuss why she left and is now forced to either find alternative housing or live on the streets. She has few options for alternative housing in Charlotte, making her thankful for Room at the Inn.

Mary is very personable with an upbeat personality. She's a licensed hairdresser and contemporary in style, which is obvious by her deep orange and purple hair arranged in an upward sweep. We register her into the system, and I ask what she wants to talk about today.

She needs a NC state ID in order to get a job. She has her Social Security card, a birth certificate, and an expired passport. The Social Security card and birth certificate will be sufficient proof of identification for the DMV. Since I don't meet many neighbors with a passport, I ask if she traveled. Yes, she says, to Europe to visit her cousin who played for a professional sports team. I give her a DMV waiver, along with the names of three local salons that may be hiring. We shake hands as she leaves and I wish her well.

# Joseph

I wonder silently about his real reason for coming in today. He gets comfortable in his chair, begins to speak slowly and choose his words carefully, as though he will be here for a while. He has to go to the lab for some blood work and plans to do it tomorrow.

"Why tomorrow? Do you have an appointment?"

"No appointment, I can go anytime."

I suggest he take the free shuttle van on Thursday, the day after tomorrow, and he quickly agrees. I'm a little surprised at how quickly he changes his mind. Maybe he was planning on taking the shuttle anyway and trying to get some bus passes to sell on the street. He's been homeless for a long time and knows bus passes are a commodity that can be bartered on the street for other things. He soon continues onto another subject, and I wait for him to get to the point.

Joseph has a warm personality and is the type of person you could enjoy talking with on a quiet afternoon. He begins discussing the book he is reading, *Escape from Hell*. He has a deep interest in its Christian subject matter and storyline and says the book has had a profound impact on him, to the point of altering his behavior and lifestyle.

"What behavior?"

"I don't want to end up in hell for eternity." This gets my mind racing. What could he have done that would make him think that? He remembers a great deal of detail about the book and seems to have a very sharp memory, but mentions no personal specifics. He says the book has given him a new perspective on breaking out of homelessness. I make a mental note to buy the book and pray it helps move him out of the cycle.

When he gets up to leave, I realize his real motive for coming wasn't as ulterior as I initially suspected. He just wanted someone to talk with.

## Summary

I was unable to discern a clear reason why this group of people were homeless at the time I met them. I suspect some were dealing with mental illness, and some had physical problems. None are easily classified. In fact, no homeless person fits into a stereotypical pigeonhole, but with the people in this chapter, I didn't have much of a clue, so I won't summarize. The stories will just have to stand on their own.

# Concluding Remarks:

Generally there are four primary obstacles the homeless have to overcome in order to climb out of the cycle. A Job, housing, food and transportation.

There aren't enough good paying jobs available for the folks I met. Most don't have skills that are marketable in the workplace and the jobs they find generally pay minimum wage. There are multiple articles and studies about this problem and no easy answers.

Housing, transportation and food are all interrelated. Many homeless live in a shelter in the center city. The available jobs are rarely close to the shelters. For those that have a job, it requires leaving the shelter before dawn to catch a bus to the site. The expense of transportation to a job on a bus can eat into a minimum wage salary quickly. Daily bus fares average 5% of a minimum wage salary. If they work odd shifts there isn't a guaranteed bed when they return to the shelter. Some wait until a bed becomes vacant to lie down. They don't have lunch food to bring with them nor the money to buy something to eat. Nutrition needs are not considered and many survive on candy bars and junk food. None of this takes into consideration other necessities such as clothing, work wear, laundry, and medical.

How to resolve these issues isn't easy but it isn't impossible. Dependency is not the answer nor is bigger government. I don't believe it's someone else's concern. Some of the answers lie in mentorship within the community, one person helping another as a mentor, friend and counselor. I also think the private sector needs to step up to the plate and designate certain jobs for the homeless. CEO's need to lead this and be supportive in order for it to work. As a volunteer with the homeless, I can honestly say I got more out of it than they did. I'm sure you will too.

CPSIA information can be obtained
at www.ICGtesting.com
Printed in the USA
BVHW031154240620
582246BV00001B/131